Jesus
Shall Reign

Revelation Simply Explained

DR. WOODROW M. KROLL

AMBASSADOR

BELFAST ◆ **GREENVILLE**
NORTHERN IRELAND   SOUTH CAROLINA

Jesus Shall Reign
© Copyright 1998 Woodrow M. Kroll

ISBN   1 84030 020   5

AMBASSADOR PUBLICATIONS
a division of
AMBASSADOR PRODUCTIONS LTD,
Providence House
16 Hillview Avenue,
Belfast, BT5 6JR
Northern Ireland

Emerald House,
1 Chick Springs Road, Suite 206
Greenville,
South Carolina 29609
United States of America

THE REVELATION OF JESUS CHRIST

Chapter 1

In the past several years there has been a great revival of interest in the future. Many people are rushing off to fraudulent fortune tellers, money-making mediums and satanic soothsayers all in an attempt to learn what will happen in the days hence. But we born-again believers need not waste our time in such fruitless activity. There is only one true source of information about the future and that is the One who holds the future in His hands — the God of the universe. If we are to know what is in store for us and this old planet, we must look to God's Word and those portions of it which foretell what one day will become history.

BLESSING PROMISED

Revelation is such a book. However, many say, "I can't understand Revelation. It's all a big puzzle to me!" Well, beloved, take heart. God knew many would close their Bibles when they reached its final chapters. Nowhere does it say we will fully understand all that is included in this wonderful, prophetic book. God doesn't expect us to understand it perfectly. He doesn't promise we will. What He does promise is found in the first chapter, the third verse. Mark this verse and remember it well. God promises, "Blessed is he that readeth, and they that hear the words of this prophecy, and keep those things which are written in it; for the time is at hand." No, we are not promised perfect understanding. But we are promised a blessing by reading the words of Revelation or hearing them and by keeping those things written therein.

This does not mean, however, that Revelation is unintelligible or that we will understand none of it. John was commanded not to seal the words of this prophecy. They were to remain open so that everyone would have opportunity to understand its contents. Rev. 22:10. If we are promised a special blessing for reading it, then apparently the book must be helpful to those who do read it.

Even the very word "Revelation" is significant. Literally it is an "apocalypse," a revealing, or an unveiling. The book is not meant to cloud our minds or to mystify but to clarify, enlighten and inform. We should expect to gain a fuller understanding of the program of God by reading the Revelation, even if we don't understand everything we read.

Therefore, as we embark on an important survey of this magnificent revelation, we seek the promised blessing of God and greater insight into what God has decreed for the future.

THE REVELATION OF JESUS CHRIST

There are several preliminary features of the book that will be helpful for us to keep in mind. The title of this writing is misleading in some Bibles. Even the King James Version denotes it as "The Revelation of St. John the Divine." Many people speak of the "Book of Revelations" in the plural. All of these are man-made titles and do not accurately convey the true purpose of the book. Verse one of chapter one is far more accurate for it is the designation given by God. We may properly refer to this writing as "The Revelation of Jesus Christ" for that is what it is. This is not a simple guide to the future, an unveiling of predicted events, but it is a grand unveiling of a person — Jesus Christ the Lord. The Revelation is a book about a person, the Saviour of men and Sovereign of the universe. Thus, we properly refer to it as "The Revelation of Jesus Christ" or "The Book of Revelation" or simply "Revelation."

THE AUTHOR

The author of this revelation is God, but the man chosen to record it for posterity was the Apostle John. The first verse of the book indicates, "The Revelation of Jesus Christ, which God gave unto him, to show unto his servants things which must shortly come to pass; and he sent and signified it by his angel unto his servant, John." This beloved disciple of the Lord was privileged in his old age to be an eyewitness to the unveiling of the events foretold in Revelation. Although some have wondered whether John was truly the man used to record this book, it appears to be certain from the fact that his name is repeated in verse four. And as if to remove all doubt and embarrass the skeptics, verse nine reads, "I, John, who also am your brother, and companion in tribulation, and in the kingdom and patience of Jesus Christ. . ." He identifies himself plainly as the human author of this account.

John continues by telling where he was when he received this revelation. Verse nine states he was in the "isle that is called Patmos, for the word of God, and for the testimony of Jesus Christ." Patmos is a tiny, wind-swept, craggy island about 35 miles southwest of the coast of Asia Minor. It was used by the Romans as a place of banishment for criminals. When John says he was there "for the word of God, and for the testimony of Jesus Christ" he doesn't mean he was sent there as a missionary. John had apparently been the pastor of the church at Ephesus and, because of his faithful and fearless preaching, the Emperor Domitian exiled him to this forsaken island. John was banished because toward the end of his reign Domitian demanded all Christians worship him as god, and instead the apostle "preached the word of God and the testimony of Jesus Christ."

DATE

We can fairly accurately place the time of the writing of Revelation by determining the date of John's exile to Patmos. The apostle did not die on Patmos but returned to his home in Ephesus, according to the Church Father Clement. Early church historian, Eusebius, says that John returned to Ephesus following the death of the Roman Emperor Domitian, who was assassinated in A.D. 96. Another Church Father, Irenaeus, claims that John lived in Ephesus after returning from Patmos until the reign of the Roman Emperor, Trajan (A.D. 98-117). This means if John was banished to Patmos during the persecution of Christians near the end of Domitian's reign (A.D. 81-96) and returned to Ephesus in A.D. 96, the recording of Revelation must have taken place about A.D. 95 or a bit earlier. Revelation, then, is the last recorded writing from the mouth of God to the pen of man.

INTERPRETATION

Since Revelation is a unique book, the only prophetic book of the New Testament, we must ask ourselves how we will interpret it. In the past, those who have studied the Bible have devised no less than four ways to view the events of Revelation.

First, there are a number of theologians who hold that nothing written in Revelation is real. They say that it is not literal but fictional. By using allegories, so these theologians say, the book simply points out spiritual lessons, mostly for encouragement. Beloved, I see little encouragement in the Great White Throne Judgment.

Second, there are those who take the position that everything recorded in this book has already been fulfilled. Adherents to this view say that the Book of Revelation records the conflicts of the early church with Judaism and paganism. They claim that, with the exception of the last two or three chapters, everything recorded was fulfilled in the fall of Jerusalem and the old Roman Empire.

Third, some say we should interpret Revelation as continuous history. They maintain the events recorded in the book cover a time span from the early church and culminate with the coming reign of Christ. Thus we are now living somewhere in the account of Revelation. But, this approach leads many people to make cockeyed identifications of present personalities with those of the Apocalypse.

It is my opinion that each of these approaches fails to fit the facts. Thus it appears that the proper method of interpreting this unveiling of the person of Christ is prophetically.

Hence, beginning with chapter four, all events recorded are yet future and will one day be fulfilled. This means that chapters four through 19 relate to the period just preceding the second coming of Christ in glory; chapter 19 refers to His coming to earth, chapter 20 to His future millennial kingdom; and chapters 21 and 22 to the events subsequent to the millennium. In our study together we shall be viewing those things "which must shortly come to pass," for the rapture of the Church, prophetically pictured in the beginning of chapter four, cannot be far off.

DIVINE OUTLINE

Although there are dozens of ways we could divide the book to aid in our study, there is none so simple, yet so profound, as the way God divides it. Chapter one, verse 19, bears the most natural, perhaps we should say supernatural, division of Revelation. John is commanded to "write the things which thou hast seen, and the things which are, and the things which shall be hereafter." Past, present and future.

The things which John hast seen are recorded in the first chapter, verses nine through 18. At verse 12, John "turned to see the voice that spoke with me." What he saw was a vision of seven candlesticks or lampstands, which are explained in verse twenty, "and in the midst of them one like the Son of man." John saw Jesus Christ dressed in His priestly garments. Verse 13. "His head and his hair were white like wool, as white as snow..." Verse 14. This is reminiscent of the Ancient of Days of Daniel's prophecy. Dan. 7:22. John saw that Jesus Christ's eyes "were like a flame of fire; And his feet like fine bronze, as if they burned in a furnace." Verses 14 and 15. The Lord had come in the fires of judgment. "Out of his mouth went a sharp two-edged sword; and his countenance was as the sun shineth in its strength." Verse 16. All of this John saw and was commanded to write.

The second division, "the things which are" is recorded in chapters two and three. These present things refer to that which takes place during the age of the Church. They include the entire Church period from its beginning to its consummation when our great God and Saviour Jesus Christ will rapture His Church.

The final division is the "things which shall be hereafter." Literally, this means the things which happen after these things, the events of chapters two and three. They are the words of prophecy which constitute the bulk of Revelation, from chapter four through the end. These chapters describe the events which will take place after the Church age has become history.

Bearing these three divisions in mind will greatly help us in understanding that which is revealed in The Revelation of Jesus Christ. "The things which thou hast seen" are gone. "The things which are" will soon come to a close and we will see before our very eyes "the things which shall be hereafter." Friends, we are living in exciting days and even a knowledge of Revelation that barely scratches the surface makes them much more exciting. Jesus is coming soon.

THE SEVEN CHURCHES

Chapters 2-3

The second division of Revelation, "the things which are," is recorded in chapters two and three. In these chapters we find seven letters. To learn of their significance, let's ask the three most important questions in tackling any interpretation of the Scriptures. Who is doing the speaking? Who is being spoken to? And what is being spoken about?

First, who is doing the speaking? The first verse of each letter gives a graphic description of the speaker. Revelation 2:1, for example, denotes the speaker as "he that holdeth the seven stars in his right hand, who walketh in the midst of the seven golden lampstands." Verse eight identifies the speaker as "the first and the last, who was dead, and is alive." In addition, 2:12,18 and 3:1,7,14 all give a description of the speaker which corresponds to the description of Christ in chapter one. The speaker to the seven churches is none other than Christ the Lord.

And to whom is Jesus Christ speaking? Each letter is addressed to "the angel" of the church. This word simply means messenger, the one who has been given authority over the churches. Probably this was the pastor through whom the message was to be delivered to the congregation. The actual identification has little bearing on the meaning of "the things which are."

The question of what is being written about brings us to the heart of these two chapters. John is told to write a letter to each of the seven churches. These were seven distinct churches which existed at that time. And yet what is so special about these churches? Why should a condition in each of these local congregations be made a part of the Revelation to the universal Church?

We must remember that Christ sent His Angel and "signi-fied" the message to John. Rev. 1:1. He used present signs to show the meaning of future events. These churches were historical congregations in western Asia Minor but they were also typical of the stages through which the universal Church would go. These local congregations signify conditions or problems that would permeate the entire Church at a later date. The complete history of the universal Church is signi-fied by conditions in the local congregations of these seven Churches of Asia. By combining these conditions we have a perfect picture of the progressive stages of the Church age.

The order in which these conditions appear in church history is exactly the same as they appear in the letters of chapters two and three. If you change the order of any one you will hopelessly confuse the facts of church history. John received the revelation of these two chapters as prophecy. Today, however, these events are mostly history. The remark-able correspondence of the conditions in these seven churches with periods of church history is certainly not acci-dental. Looking back on nineteen hundred years of the church, we are simply amazed at the appropriateness of the order of events and the accuracy of their fulfillment.

Let's consider the seven churches and the stages of church history they represent.

EPHESUS (2:2-7)

This city was the capital of Asia Minor, where John resided both before and after receiving the Revelation on Patmos. The church was established by Paul on his third missionary journey. Acts 19. The word Ephesus means "desirable" and is the endearing term a young Greek lad would use to refer to his bride-to-be. How appropriate. When Christ left His Church in the world it was as a chaste virgin, the Bride of Christ, espoused to the Bridegroom. It is likely the Ephesian church represents the Apostolic Era or the first century church.

This was an evangelistic church which had labored for the Master. 2:2-3. It was a separated church for it could "not bear them who are evil." 2:2. It was an orthodox church which "tried them who say they are apostles, and are not and hast found them liars." 2:2. It was a people's church that "hatest the deeds of the Nicolaitans." 2:6. (These, whose name means "conquerors of the people," were a group who argued that there ought to be two classes in the church — clergy and laity. They wanted a hierarchy to rule the church.) But alas, Ephesus was a church that had lost its "first love." Their emotional fervor and depth of love for God had waned. They no longer spontaneously expressed their love and devotion to God as they once had.

SYMRNA (2:8-11)

Smyrna means "myrrh" which is an aromatic substance that comes from a thorny tree but must be crushed in order to yield its perfume and fragrance. How appropriately this speaks of the second period of church history, the second- and third-century church. Persecutions began before the end of the Apostolic Age, but in the next two centuries the persecutions of the Roman government were directed at the church like the crushing of myrrh. At no time in the history of the church was such a fragrance of faithfulness and loyalty to Christ yielded under such intense persecution. Yet each crushing blow gave a "sweet-smelling savour unto God."

PERGAMOS (2:12-17)

The period symbolized by the Church at Pergamos carries us to about the year A.D. 500. Pergamos is a picture of the church in compromise. This city was an important religious center where the pagan cults of Athena, Zeus, Asclepius and Dionysus were prominent. Here too was a university and a large library of two-hundred thousand volumes, later sent to Egypt as a gift from Antony to Cleopatra. The word

Pergamos means "marriage" and signifies the spiritual adultery which this church engaged in. What the devil could not do by Roman persecution in the preceding period, he tried to do by patronage in this period. Outward assault made the church grow inwardly stronger. Thus Satan switched his tactics from persecution to protection. During this period the church became an official institution of the state. State taxes supported it and paid its pastors. The leavening of the pure church had already begun. The doctrine of Balaam was being spread, which resulted in a union of the church and the world. The Nicolaitan tendencies present in the Church of Ephesus had now become doctrine in the Church of Pergamos. The clergy ruled the laity and a papal system arose which led to the hierarchy of Romanism.

THYATIRA (2:18-29)

The Church of Thyatira symbolizes the period from A.D. 500 to 1500. As the worldliness of the Church at Pergamos led to the papacy, so too the Church at Thyatira introduced other excesses which would become dominant in the church. Thyatira means "continual sacrifice." How fitting this name is — for in this period was invented the doctrine that every time the priest performed the mass, the wafer turned into the actual body of Christ and the wine turned into His literal blood. The continual sacrifice of Christ is a damnable heresy which puts our Lord to shame. Heb. 6:6. Symbolic representation of this is made by the introduction of Jezebel in verse 20. As this heathen princess endeavored to unite Judaism with her own pagan religion, so too many ungodly practices and excesses have attempted to prostitute the teachings which the church inherited from Jesus Christ. The Church of Thyatira represents the enlargement of the seeds of corruption which the devil earlier introduced into the church.

SARDIS (3:1-6)

Sardis, which means "remnant," is the perfect representation of the church in reformation. Having recognized the abuses so prevalent in the church for over one thousand years, and having become convinced that "the just shall live by faith," Martin Luther lifted his hand against Roman tyranny in Germany. Across the continent others joined him in attempting to reform their beloved church. Protestantism was born and the seeds of corruption were badly bruised. The remnant in the church who "have not defiled their garments" (verse 4) sought a return to the "pure religion and undefiled" which the apostles had known. This brought about the Protestant Reformation.

PHILADELPHIA (3:7-13)

The sixth message of Jesus Christ is the one to the Church of Philadelphia. This church symbolically marks the great revival period of the eighteenth and nineteenth centuries. Revelation 3:7-8 depicts this as the church with an open door. Our Lord commended the Philadelphians for using the opportunities of evangelism afforded by the open door, for keeping His Word, and for their separation and fidelity. In church history this signifies the years of Spurgeon, Wesley, Whitfield, Moody, etc. There was a great spiritual awakening and everywhere doors were being opened to the Gospel.

LAODICEA (3:14-19)

Now we come to the final state of the church, the Church at Laodicea. The word Laodicea means "the people's rights" and if ever there was a day when people are clamoring for equal rights it is today. With respect to the church, people themselves have taken over the church and the Lord is no longer the head. Conventions, denominations, councils, etc., governed by people now run the church. Verse 16 says the members of this church were "neither cold nor hot." No one accused them of the excesses which characterized the church centuries before. However, no one could accuse them of serving the Lord zealously either. Because their works were neither hot nor cold they made the Lord sick; He said, "I will spew thee out of my mouth."

Beloved, there is no doubt in my mind that we are living in this very period of church history symbolically portrayed by the Church of Laodicea. We don't have to worry about atheism, communism or liberalism. What we have to worry about is pussy-footism. We have to worry about straddling the fence and getting bogged down in the things of this world which prohibit us from serving Jesus Christ zealously. This was the problem at Laodicea. It is our problem today.

Verse nineteen indicates the Lord's reason for delivering these seven messages. He says, "As many as I love, I rebuke and chasten; be zealous, therefore, and repent." We have been on the road a long time since the days of the early church but I wonder how far we have come. The Lord's command to the twentieth-century church is the same as His command to the Laodicean Church; be zealous, therefore, and repent. I'm afraid we've become ill with the same sickness.

Read to here - Bill
2006 -
august 10

THE THINGS
WHICH SHALL BE HEREAFTER

Chapters 4-5

We now embark on a long journey into the future. In relation to the divinely inspired outline of Revelation 1:19, we are about to chart a course in "the things which shall be hereafter." From the standpoint of the twentieth century, all that occurs in the Revelation from this time on will be future. Beginning with chapter four, things to come are unfolded. Chapters four and five are the introduction and background to the broad scope of prophetic events in the rest of the book. To some degree they provide a table of contents for the chapters that follow.

RAPTURE SIGNIFIED

Revelation 4:1 reads, "After this I looked and, behold, a door was opened in heaven; and the first voice that I heard was, as it were, of a trumpet talking with me; which said, Come up here, and I will show thee things which must be hereafter." The striking similarities between the elements of this verse and those of I Thessalonians 4:13-18, which record the rapture of the Church cannot be coincidence. Here, as a representative of the Church, John envisions being caught up into heaven to view the future. This even symbolizes the catching up to heaven of all born-again believers before judgment begins. That this is a sign of the rapture of the Church (those who have received Jesus Christ as Saviour) is believed for the following reasons:

1. Beginning with 4:1, the word "church" does not appear again in Revelation until 22:16, after judgment is finished.

2. There is an obvious transition between chapters three and four. Chapter three speaks of the churches; chapter

four of judgment. Chapter three is set on earth; chapter four in heaven. Chapter three closes the division of "the things which are"; chapter four opens the division of "the things which shall be hereafter."

3. The first vision of Christ in Revelation pictures Him in the midst of the seven lampstands (which the book itself interprets as the seven churches). But in chapters 4-19, Christ is pictured in heaven. 4:1-2, 5:5-6. It is certainly logical to believe the Church is there with Him. John 14:1-3.

4. The promise made to the Philadelphian Church was that it would be kept from the hour of trial. Rev. 3:10. In order to escape the terrible judgment of Revelation 4-19, the Church must be translated to heaven before that time. I Thess. 1:9-10; 5:9.

For these and many other reasons, it appears that John's vision of himself being caught up from earth to heaven is a symbolic representation of the rapture of the Church before the events of the Tribulation described in chapters 4-19.

THE THRONE OF GOD

The first thing John envisions in heaven is a throne. This is not symbolism, but a judgment scene set in heaven. This throne is neither the Great White Throne of Revelation 20:11 nor the Judgment Seat of Christ of II Corinthians 5:10. The one sitting on the throne is none other than God Himself. This is clear from the symbolism of verses three and five and from the direct reference to God in verse eight. John's senses are immediately struck by the person on the throne. Verse three records, "And he that sat was to look upon like a jasper and a sardius stone ..." The jasper stone, explained in Revelation 21:11, is a crystal-clear white stone representing the purity and glory of God. On the other hand, the sardius stone is ruby colored, a blood red. By this is pictured God's redemptive nature.

The throne itself has an emerald colored rainbow completely encircling it and out of the throne proceed lightnings and thunderings. Verses 3,5. Here again is a contrasting picture of God. This is a throne of judgment, depicted by the lightning and thunder. But mingled with God's righteous judgment is His mercy, represented by the rainbow. Gen. 9:13-16.

TWENTY-FOUR ELDERS

Those around the throne of God are equally interesting. Verse four relates, "And round about the throne were four and twenty thrones, and upon the thrones I saw four and twenty elders sitting, clothed in white raiment; and they had on their heads crowns of gold." The seats upon which these 24 elders sit are thrones which indicate they are given positions of authority. Who can these elders be? The most logical identification is that they are the raptured Church. They are representative of the entire Church. As the officials of the Church today, no better symbol than the elders could be used in this vision to represent the whole Church. Acts 15:6;20:17; James 5:14.

The activity of the 24 elders gives us a clue as to our own activity in heaven. Verse 4. The elders rise and prostrate themselves before God and worship Him. Verse 10. To worship means to ascribe honor to and that is exactly what the elders do when they say, "Thou art worthy, O Lord, to receive glory and honor and power; for thou hast created all things, and for thy pleasure they are and were created." Verse 11.

Another activity of the elders is seen in verse ten. Here they cast their crowns before the throne as they praise the Lord. These are not diadems or crowns of royalty. They are the crowns that have been won in the arena of faith. They are the crowns of faithful service during this life. What better way to praise and honor God than to cast at His feet the tangible evidence of our heavenly reward.

LIVING CREATURES

There is one more group around the throne that needs identification. They are the four beasts, or as the word is more correctly translated "living ones" or "living creatures." Verses 6-7. These are not grotesque animals but rather living creatures of diverse characteristics. The first is like a lion, the second like a calf, the third has a face like a man, and the fourth is like a flying eagle. Each of them has six wings and are "full of eyes" which depicts their incessant activity in praising the Lord.

These four living creatures are heavenly cherubim. Ezekiel writes of living creatures and identifies them as cherubim. Ezek. 10:15,20. They complete the symbolism that every living creature in heaven will praise God, both earthly and heavenly beings. These four living ones "rest not day and night, saying, Holy, holy, holy, Lord God Almighty, who was, and is, and is to come." Verse 8. Both the raptured Church, represented by the 24 elders, and the heavenly angels, represented by the four living cherubim, will one day praise the Lord as He ought to be praised today.

THE SCROLL

Chapter five finds John viewing another majestic sight. In the right hand of God, sitting on the throne, is a book which has been written upon both inside and out. In the days of John, books were usually scrolls rather than leafbooks as we have today. When a scroll was completely filled with writing, it would be rolled a little way, a seal placed on it, rolled a little more and sealed again. When it was completely rolled, there would be seven seals securing its message. To unroll the scroll and reveal the contents, the seals must be successively broken.

This sealed scroll recalls the ancient Jewish custom of the kinsman-redeemer. Ruth 4. Under the Law, when an owner of property allowed another to take possession of it, a sort of mortgage deed was given to the original property owner. This was a sealed scroll which stated that at some future date a kinsman or heir could reclaim that property if the purchase price was met. The land owner's representative must be a legal kinsman and be worthy of the right to purchase the property. When he had paid the stated purchase price, then, and only then, could he break the seals on the scroll. This worthy seal-breaker was called the "redeemer" for he had regained the property from the hands of another.

THE SEARCH

But here a grave problem arises. John sees a mighty angel proclaiming in a loud voice, "Who is worthy to open the scroll, and to loose its seals?" Rev. 5:2. Since this is the title deed to the universe and only the purchaser of redemption can receive it from the hand of God, an intensive search is made to discover a man worthy to open the scroll. Verse three indicates that though heaven, earth and the nether world are searched, no man worthy is found. By sin all men have forfeited their worthiness to open the scroll.

This caused John to fall into uncontrollable despair and much weeping. No man was found worthy to receive the scroll from the hand of God. Was this to be the end of the revelation? Was it possible that the scroll would have to remain sealed and its message unknown?

THE LAMB

Suddenly one of the elders said to the greatly sorrowful John, "Weep not; behold, the Lion of the tribe of Judah, the Root of David, hath prevailed to open the scroll, and to loose its seven seals." Verse 5. Then John looked up and "in the midst of the throne and of the four living creatures, and in the midst of the elders, stood a Lamb as though it had been slain, having seven horns and seven eyes, which are the seven spirits of God sent forth unto all the earth. And he came and took the scroll out of the right hand of him that sat upon the throne." Verses 6-7.

Here was the answer to the angel's question, "Who is worthy to open the scroll, and to loose its seals?" The Lamb is worthy. The Lion of the tribe of Judah has qualified Himself to open the scroll. This is none other than the Lion (Gen. 49:10) from between the feet of Judah, and the Root of David (Isa. 11:1), the Prince of Peace (Isa. 9:6-7), the Lamb of God. John 1:29. This is Jesus Christ the Lord. The title deed is in the hand of God and only Jesus has paid the purchase price. He has purchased all things by His death on Calvary. Since Jesus Christ alone has paid the price for redeeming God's property, He is the only one who is able to take the scroll out of the hands of God. On the cross the title to the redeemed souls of the universe was purchased with Christ Jesus' blood and now He steps up and receives the scroll in one of the most dramatic scenes of history. Jesus Christ, the Redeemer, claims those for whom He has died and immediately the four living creatures and 24 elders sing a new song, a song of praise to the Redeemer. They sing, "Thou art worthy to take the scroll, and to open its seals; for thou wast slain, and hast redeemed us to God by thy blood out of every kindred, and tongue, and people, and nation; And hast made us unto our God a kingdom of priests, and we shall reign on the earth." Rev. 5:9-10. Even the angels ten thousand times ten thousand strong, who could not sing the new song of redemption, join in the celebration of praise to the one worthy to receive the scroll by saying with a loud voice, "Worthy is the Lamb that was slain to receive power, and riches, and wisdom, and strength, and honor, and glory, and blessing." Verse 12.

Finally every creature in heaven, on earth and under the earth sing honor and blessing to the Lamb. Yes, Christ Jesus humbled Himself, came to earth in the form of a man and died for you and me. "Wherefore God also hath highly exalted him, and given him a name which is above every name, That at the name of Jesus every knee should bow, of things in heaven, and things in earth, and things under the earth, And that every tongue should confess that Jesus Christ is Lord, to the glory of God, the Father." Phil. 2:9-11. Beloved, this is exactly what will happen when the worthy Lamb receives the title deed to the universe from God the Father. As believers, we will be there to witness this great event. I wouldn't miss it for the world.

Bill 7-25-06
Tuesday

—18—

THE SEVEN SEALS

Chapters 6-7

Beginning with the sixth chapter and continuing all the way to chapter nineteen, the Apostle John is permitted to view the Tribulation period. Within these important chapters are a series of three judgments — the seals (6), the trumpets (8-9) and the bowls (16). Between the record of each judgment is a parenthetical chapter or chapters, which provide additional information about each judgment. For example, the judgment of the seals in chapter six is elaborated upon in chapter seven.

You'll recall that the seals are placed on the title deed to the universe which only the worthy Redeemer, Jesus Christ, is legally able to open. This is a transaction between Father and Son; the Father is the property owner and the Son its redeemer. Jesus Christ paid the redemption price with His own life's blood and now He is fully qualified to open the seals and enter into the possession of His property. With the opening of these seals is ushered in the Tribulation, the 70th week of Daniel. Dan. 9:24-27. Let us see the future revealed as each of the seals is successively broken by the worthy Redeemer.

THE FIRST SEAL (6:1-2)

At the opening of the first seal by the Lamb of God, the first of the four horsemen of the Apocalypse is revealed to John. The rider held a bow, wore a crown and went "forth conquering, and to conquer."

The appearance of the white horse makes one think of the white horse in Revelation 19:11. But the rider revealed by the first seal cannot be Christ, for He is the one who holds

— 19 —

the scroll and opens the seal. No, this is not Christ, but one who comes in the name of Christ (Matt. 24:5), masquerading as the Christ. He is the Antichrist and therefore comes saying, "Peace, peace," offering a plan of world peace and promising a false Millennium. But you remember Paul said, "When they shall say, Peace and safety; then sudden destruction cometh upon them, as travail upon a woman with child; and they shall not escape." I Thess. 5:3. This false christ (II Thess. 2:3-12) is the Man of Sin, the covenant making prince of Daniel 9:26.

THE SECOND SEAL (6:3-4)

With the opening of the second seal a red horse appears. This signifies the second phase of the reign of Antichrist. Having come in peace, he soon plunges the whole world into bloodshed. "And there went out another horse that was red; and power was given to him that sat on it to take peace from the earth . . . and there was given unto him a great sword." Verse 4. The peace plan offered by the Antichrist and so readily accepted by the nations of this world will now be withdrawn and he will cause world-wide war and bloodshed.

THE THIRD SEAL (6:5-6)

When the third seal is opened, a black horse appears and its rider has a pair of balances in his hand. Following closely on the heels of war will be famine and starvation. "And I heard a voice in the midst of the four living creatures say, A measure of wheat for a denarius, and three measures of barley for a denarius, and see thou hurt not the oil and the wine." Verse 6. The balances suggest that a system of rationing will be enforced. Rev. 13:16-17. In New Testament times a denarius or a penny was one day's wages and bought only enough for one person. Matt. 20:2,9. Due to the devastation of war, the production of grain will be greatly curtailed and the whole world will have to ration its food. Beloved, we are heading that way now.

THE FOURTH SEAL (6:7-8)

The last horseman of the Apocalypse rides a pale horse and the rider's name is Death. Actually the word "pale" means green-like, as a corpse. This rider, Death, will exterminate those living on the earth by four means: sword (war), hunger (famine), death (plagues which accompany famine) and wild beasts (which will roam unrestrained).

THE FIFTH SEAL (6:9-11)

The fifth seal depicts the souls of those "slain for the Word of God, and for the testimony which they held." These cannot be the martyrs of the Church Age for they were raptured before the holocaust of opening the seals. They must be those martyred for their faith during the first months of the Tribulation. Their being under the altar is symbolic of the fact that these people have been purchased by the blood of Christ. When they inquire how long it will be until the Lord avenges their blood, they are told to rest with their fellow servants and brethren for many more will yet join the ranks of the slain.

THE SIXTH SEAL (6:12-17)

With the breaking of the sixth seal, havoc is unleashed on the earth and the Lord's wrath brings cataclysmic judgment. Six literal, catastrophic events will occur: (1) a great earthquake, (2) the sun becomes black, (3) the moon becomes reddened like blood, (4) a universal meteor shower of stars falls to earth, (5) the heavens part as a scroll revealing God on His awesome throne, and (6) every mountain and island are moved when the heavens roll back. The result will be panic and fear when men "hid themselves in the dens and in the rocks of the mountains, And said to the mountains and the rocks, Fall on us, and hide us from the face of him that sitteth on the throne, and from the wrath of the Lamb. Verses 15-16.

RESTRAINING JUDGMENT

Before the opening of the seventh seal, some additional information about this period of Tribulation is provided for us in chapter seven. Here John sees four angels standing on the four corners of the earth, holding the four winds of the earth. The "fours" here represent the universality of these angels' activity. Revelation 7:2-3 depicts a fifth and apparently superior angel arising out of the east and instructing the four angels to "hurt not the earth, neither the sea, nor the trees, till we have sealed the servants of our God in their foreheads." Verse 3. These angels are restraining judgment long enough to reveal God's grace. They are holding on to the winds of God's judgment so that He may save two great throngs of people during this Tribulation period.

THE 144,000

The first group God chooses to save are "sealed" during the first three and one-half years of the Tribulation. Verses 3-8. The purpose of the seal is to indicate ownership and the reference to their foreheads suggests that they are publicly known as the saved of God.

The number to be sealed is 144,000 and God's revelation to John clearly indicates that this group of 144,000 is composed of 12,000 from each of the twelve tribes of Israel. Mark it down, friends, the 144,000 are JEWS. The constant repetition of the phrase "of the tribe of . . . were sealed" is too forceful to allow any other logical conclusion.

Those today who claim to be among this group would have to know which tribe they belonged to and since all such tribal records were destroyed when the Roman General Titus sacked Jerusalem in A.D. 70 there is not a person alive today who can honestly and Biblically claim to be a part of the 144,000. Besides, most who claim to be included in this number are not even Jews and God's Word clearly indicates that the 144,000 of God's sealed servants will be out of Israel.

THE GREAT MULTITUDE

Because this vast number of Jewish servants faithfully witness to the saving power of Christ Jesus, a second group of individuals is saved while the angels withhold God's impending judgment. Revelation 7:9 records, "After this I beheld and, lo, a great multitude, which no man could number, of all nations, and kindreds, and peoples, and tongues, stood before the throne, and before the Lamb, clothed with white robes, and palms in their hands."

As the 144,000 were all Jews, here is a great multitude of saved people who are of all nations, all tribes, all peoples and tongues. They stand before the Lamb in white robes indicating that they too have been saved by the blood of the Lamb. Along with all the angels and the twenty-four elders, representing the Church, this great multitude praises the God of our salvation and the Lamb.

To John's question concerning the origin of this numberless multitude, one of the elders gives the noteworthy answer, "These are they who came out of the great tribulation, and have washed their robes, and made them white in the blood of the Lamb." Verse 14. As the 144,000 were sealed during the first part of the Tribulation, so too these are saved during the last part. What a wonderful picture of God's mercy. Although the Tribulation is a time of judgment yet it will be a time of salvation as well. An election out of Israel will be redeemed with an innumerable multitude of Gentiles. Isn't God gracious? In the midst of justice is found His salvation, for through the Tribulation come those who have been washed in the blood of the Lamb.

A FINAL WARNING

Now, you may say, "Well, if multitudes are going to be saved during the Tribulation, then I'll just wait. I don't need to be born again now. After the rapture, I'll get my heart right with the Lord."

Friend, I have bad news for you. No one who hears the Gospel today and rejects it will have an opportunity to be saved during the Tribulation. II Thessalonians 2:11-12 says, "And for this cause God shall send them strong delusion, that they should believe the lie, That they all might be judged who believed not the truth, but had pleasure in unrighteousness." If you reject the Gospel today you will become a victim of the strong delusion spread by the Antichrist during the Tribulation. You will swallow his lie hook, line and sinker whether you want to or not. As a result, you will not believe the truth of the Gospel then and will be damned because you reject Christ now. Only those who have not fully understood the Gospel story or who have never heard it will have opportunity to believe it during the Tribulation. These will be the multitudes saved in Revelation seven.

With this in mind, each of you should examine yourself to see whether or not you are of the faith. Jesus Christ died for you in payment for your sin. If you reject His payment, you will have to pay for your sin yourself. The Bible says, **"For the wages of sin is death, but the gift of God is eternal life through Jesus Christ, our Lord."** Rom. 6:23. Receive Jesus and eternal life is yours. Reject Him and eternal death is yours. I have placed the message of the Gospel and Jesus the slain Lamb of the Gospel in your hands. What will you do with Him?

THE SEVEN TRUMPETS

Chapters 8-9

THE SEVENTH SEAL

As the interlude of chapter seven comes to a close, the first verse of Revelation eight brings us to another crisis event. "And when he had opened the seventh seal, there was silence in heaven about the space of half an hour." Six seals have been opened previously and judgment has poured forth. Now the last of the seals is opened and is followed by an amazing response. There is immediately an ominous hush throughout heaven. Moments before the whole company of angels, living creatures and elders were engaged in tumultuous praise of the One sitting on the throne and of the Lamb of God. Now suddenly there is silence so intense you can feel it. The final seal has been torn away from the title deed to the universe and the calamities about to be witnessed are so awful that the company of heaven is speechless. This is the calm before the storm and lasts for a full thirty minutes. If the coming judgment is so intense that the angels silently gasp in horror, how much more should men be alarmed at this terrible judgment and rush to be cleansed by the blood of the Lamb.

As the vision continues, John is shown seven angels who stand before God and receive seven trumpets. Verse 2. These are special angels for they are called "the" seven angels, a distinct group for a distinct purpose. They are marked by special power, dignity and service. Heb. 1:7,14. The trumpets are instruments of proclamation. The sounding of the trumpet is always followed by an outstanding announcement or event. Ex. 19:16;20:18; Jer. 4:5; I Cor. 15:51-52; I Thess. 4:16.

Before the trumpets can be sounded, another angel appears, standing before the altar with a gold censer and much incense. This probably refers to Christ Jesus in His office as High Priest. The incense, symbolic of the finished work of Christ, causes smoke to rise to the throne of God along with the prayers of the saints. The reason our prayers have any efficacy at all is because of the sweet savor of Christ's life and work on Calvary in our behalf. Once prayer ascends, judgment descends. The fire, verse five, represents judgment as do the thunder, lightning and earthquake. The seven angels are now ready to sound the seven trumpets proclaiming judgment.

THE FIRST TRUMPET (8:7)

As the first trumpet is blown, John sees hail and fire mixed with blood fiercely falling to the earth. So great is the devastation that one third of the earth's trees and green grass is completely burned up. Friends, this is a literal burning up of one third of the earth's vegetation. There is no reason to assume this to be figurative since we take the plagues of Egypt to be literal. Ex. 9:23-24.

THE SECOND TRUMPET (8:8-9)

The second angel sounds a trumpet and "as it were, a great mountain burning with fire" was cast into the sea. It is not necessary that we identify this instrument of judgment with anything in our present realm of experience. It may be a meteoric mass blazing from the sky and falling headlong into the sea. It may be some atomic reaction. Whatever it is, the destruction caused is unbelievable. One third of the sea turns to blood, one third of the marine life is annihilated by this fiery mass, and one third of the ships is destroyed. This will not be any time to be on a pleasure cruise.

THE THIRD TRUMPET (8:10-11)

As the trumpet of the third angel sounds, there "fell a great star from heaven, burning as though it were a lamp." Perhaps a meteor, a great glowing body will fall to earth and destroy another third of the world's water supply, including underground sources of water. Turning sweet water bitter, this judgment will mean that now two thirds of the world's water will be deadly poison. This bitter star is given the name Wormwood. A species of plant related to our sagebrush, Wormwood is always used as a symbol of bitterness. It makes a liquor which leads to mental deterioration and death. From drinking the waters poisoned by the star Wormwood, men will go out of their minds and die in judgment.

THE FOURTH TRUMPET (8:12-13)

The judgment of the fourth trumpet causes one third of the sun to be blackened, one third of the moon, and one third of all the stars. There will be a great decrease in the amount of light and in the time that reduced light is visible. Hours of light during both day and night will also be reduced by one third.

Notice the progression of the judgments stemming from the trumpets. First affected will be the trees and grass, then one third of marine life and shipping. Next one third of the pure water and finally one third of the heavenly bodies, both in respect to quantity and time. This means that not only is the small amount of food available partially destroyed, but in addition, transportation and means of food distribution are hampered, water for increased food growth is limited and precious light necessary for food production and harvesting is curtailed. Beloved, these will be dark days in more than one sense of the word.

But if you think this is a bleak picture, you haven't seen anything yet. Recorded in verse 13, John spies an angel, more correctly translated an eagle, flying through the heaven and crying in a loud voice, **"Woe, woe, woe, to the inhabiters of the earth by reason of the other voices of the trumpet of the three angels, which are yet to sound!"** No question about it. The severity of judgment is becoming noticeably greater.

THE FIFTH TRUMPET (9:1-12)

With the blowing of the fifth trumpet, we see the reason for the eagle saying, "Woe, woe, woe, to the inhabiters of the earth . . ." This trumpet entails the first of these three woes.

Revelation 9:1 records that John saw a "star fall from heaven unto the earth; and to him was given the key of the bottomless pit." The word "fall" is really "fallen." Thus, John did not see the star as it fell but saw an already fallen star. The fact that this star is given the key to the bottomless pit must mean it is a being and not an inanimate heavenly body. The Bible frequently uses "star" as a symbol of an angel. Rev. 1:20. Who is this star? He is the angel over the bottomless pit whose name in Hebrew is Abaddon and in Greek is Apollyon. Verse 11. Both of these names mean destroyer. This angel is the king over those of the bottomless pit, a fallen star of supreme authority. This is Lucifer, the son of the morning (morning star) who was cast out of heaven to the ground for the pride in his heart. Isa. 14:12-15. Satan is the fallen star.

But note, when Satan opens the pit, smoke arises out of it like the smoke of a great furnace and the sun is darkened by the black, smoky air. Out of the smoke come locusts who have been given the power of scorpions. The physical appearance of these locusts is extremely gross. They are like horses prepared for battle, having crowns on their heads, with faces like men and hair like women, but teeth like a lion. They will wear breastplates of iron and the sound of their wings will be like the sound of chariots rushing into battle. Their tails will be like scorpions' tails with the power to sting severely and torment those they do sting five months.

Given the title locusts because they perform a similar function as these marauding pests, those loosed out of the bottomless pit by their leader, Satan, are actually demons. They gravely torment those who do not have the seal of God in their foreheads. These tormented ones are driven to sorceries, witchcraft, fornication, murders, thefts and other results of pagan idolatry and demon worship and possession. Here we have the perfect final fulfillment of I Timothy 4:1-3 which predicts the outbreak of demonic worship in the time of the end.

THE SIXTH TRUMPET (9:13-21)

One woe is past but two are yet to come. The sixth angelic trumpeter sounds out, "Loose the four angels who are bound in the great river, Euphrates." The River Euphrates was considered to be the eastern extremity of the Roman Empire and the dividing line between east and west. Thus, the four loosened angels lead an army arising out of the east. These four wicked angels cannot move but at the command of God. When they are loosed and given permission to move, however, the army of horsemen they lead numbers 200,000,000. This is an almost inconceivable number. At peak strength during World War II, the United States only had 12,400,000 soldiers. But considering the hordes of the east, this number of horsemen could easily be reached today. This horrible army destroys one third of the populace. Rev. 9:15. Remember, under the fourth seal judgment (6:4) one fourth of the earth had been slain. Now, one third is slain. This means that these two judgments alone, not to mention the multitudes who have died due to famine, poisoned water, etc., have reduced the population of the earth by one half since the beginning of the Tribulation.

Whether this mighty army, with its horses having heads like lions, tails like serpents, and fire, smoke and brimstone issuing out of their mouths, should be considered all human, all demon, equipped with modern weapons of war or not, is not really important. What is important is the world's reaction to the deadly judgment of the sixth trumpet. Revelation 9:20-21 records, "And the rest of the men who were not killed by these plagues yet repented not of the works of their hands, that they should not worship demons, and idols of gold, and silver, and bronze, and stone, and wood, which neither can see, nor hear, nor walk. Neither repented they of their murders, nor of their sorceries, nor of their fornication, nor of their thefts."

In spite of the awful judgment inflicted on the world by this invading army, those who survive are still unrepentant. Such is typical of the hardened human heart. They still live in sin and debauchery, they still worship demons and idols, they still murder, practice drug abuse, fornicate and steal. Beloved, without the redeeming power of God in a person's life, there is no difference between these unfortunate inhabitants and the inhabitants of our planet today. The heart is still deceitful and desperately wicked. Jer. 17:9. Whether living in Old Testament times, New Testament times, the twentieth century or the Tribulation, all men everywhere need to repent and receive the precious blood of Jesus as an atonement for their sins. Without it, there is no hope.

THE TWO WITNESSES

Chapters 10-11

With the beginning of chapter 10 comes another parenthetical section providing additional information about the events of the Tribulation period. This parenthesis, like that of chapter seven, does not move the narrative forward but simply adds detail to the events of this time of judgment.

THE SUN-FACED ANGEL

In the first verse, John is permitted to see still another mighty angel. The physical appearance of this angel is significant. The angel originates in heaven, is clothed with a cloud, has a rainbow upon his head, a face like the sun and feet like pillars of fire. Many have thought this angel to be Christ. This is unlikely however. Crying with the voice of a roaring lion, the angel stands upon the sea and upon the earth showing his authority in all the earth, but his authority is apparently not his own. He swears by "him that liveth forever and ever, who created heaven and the things that are in it, and the earth and the things that are in it, and the sea and the things which are in it . . ." Verse 6. In swearing by the Creator, Jesus Christ, this angel shows that he has come in our Lord's authority but is not the Lord Himself.

In the hand of this angel is a little, previously opened scroll. It is not the seven-sealed scroll but a much smaller book. John is commanded to "Seal up those things which the seven thunders uttered, and write them not." Verse 4.

When the seventh angel shall sound his trumpet then the mystery of God will begin to be known and this sun-faced angel is anxious that there be no delay (time) before it is sounded. The sounding of the seventh trumpet marks the commencement of the end of the age and all that was revealed by God through His Old Testament prophets and all the mysteries of the kingdom of Christ will be known.

THE BITTER SWEET BOOK

At this point John is commanded to take the little book and eat it. The command to eat the scroll is reminiscent of the similar experiences of Ezekiel (Ezek. 2:9-10; 3:1-4,14) and Jeremiah (Jer. 15:16-18). This is a symbolic way of saying that John is to devour its contents, become thoroughly familiar with it, assimilate it, digest its meaning. This we should be doing with the Word of God each day.

But notice that the message of this book will be bitter sweet. Verse 9. John is delighted with a new revelation but is disturbed with the nature of that revelation. He rejoices in the final glory that will be his Lord's but grieves that so much more judgment must precede the final glory.

MEASURING THE TEMPLE

Chapter 11 continues the parenthetical information about the time of the seven trumpets. The chapter begins with John's recording, "And there was given me a reed like a rod; and the angel stood, saying, Rise, and measure the temple of God, and the altar, and them that worship in it. But the court, which is outside the temple, leave out, and measure it not; for it is given unto the nations, and the holy city shall they tread under foot forty and two months." The rod is a reed of the common type grown in the Jordan Valley; it is lightweight, probably 10 or 12 feet long and ideal for a measuring reed. John is told to measure the temple, the altar and even the worshipers. This temple is the one which will be rebuilt in Jerusalem; the same temple in which the man of sin will demand to be worshiped and overthrow Jewish worship. II Thess. 2:4. The measuring is an act of claiming or staking out. It is symbolic of God's possession of the temple. The fact that even the worshipers are measured indicates that God is beginning again to deal with the nation Israel. This is definitely Daniel's 70th week. Dan. 9:27.

However, the angel specifically instructs John not to measure the court of the temple for it is outside the holy place and given to the nations who shall tread it under foot forty and two months. Here is that familiar phrase "forty and two months" which is also expressed as "time, times and a half" (Rev. 12:14), "a thousand two hundred and three-score days" (Rev. 11:3), or 3½ years. All of these expressions indicate the last half of the seven-year Tribulation period. Here in 11:2 we are told that the Gentiles will tread the outer court and the city under foot for 3½ years after the covenant of peace with Israel is broken. Dan. 9:27.

THE TWO WITNESSES

At this time chronologically, the Lord's power or authority will be given to two witnesses. Verse 3. During the first half of the Tribulation God's spokesmen are the 144,000 sealed servants of Israel. However, after these servants finish their ministry and flee to the mountains (12:6), God does not leave this earth without a messenger of the Gospel. Two powerful preachers are raised up at the middle of the Tribulation period and prophesy 1,260 days or 3½ years. It is the ministry of these two preachers which incites the wrath of Antichrist. These witnesses are clothed in sackcloth and are said to be "the two olive trees, and the two lampstands standing before the God of the earth." Rev. 11:4. The figure of olive trees is brought over from Zechariah 4:3,14 and simply means that they are anointed ones. The figure of the two candlesticks or lampstands refers to the witnesses' character as the bearers of God's light in the dark days of judgment.

THEIR IDENTIFICATION

It is not possible to say dogmatically who these two witnesses are. They may possibly be just two saints who arise from those who turn to Christ in the days following the rapture. Perhaps they are converts of the 144,000. But too, these witnesses strangely fit the descriptions and characteristics of two prior prophets of God. Elijah is a good possibility for the identification of one of them. Mal. 4:4-6; James 5:17-18; I Kings 17:1, etc. Perhaps the other is

Moses. Mal. 4:4; Matt. 17:4; II Peter 1:16; Ex. 7:20; 9:14. Or Enoch may be a candidate for the identification of the other witness. Jude 14-15; Heb. 11:5.

Whoever these two great preachers are, their ministry for the Lord is outstanding. They will have power (1) to kill their enemies with fire, (2) keep it from raining, (3) turn the waters to blood, and (4) bring plagues upon the earth. Verses 5-6. The first two powers make us think of Elijah, the last two of Moses.

MURDER AND HATRED

However, at last the ministry of these two great prophets will come to an abrupt and brutal end. When they have finished their ministry **"the beast that ascendeth out of the bottomless pit shall make war against them, and shall overcome them, and kill them."** Verse 7. Please note, beloved, absolutely nothing happens to these two witnesses until they **"have finished their testimony."** They are invincible up to that point. Nothing can thwart the purposes of God. But, as in the case of many other great prophets of God, when their ministry is finished, God permits their enemy to overcome them.

As if their murder isn't enough for this godless beast, he also allows their dead bodies to lie in the street of that great city of Jerusalem, here spiritually characterized by Sodom and Egypt. Verse 8. (Sodom stands for moral corruption, Egypt for the spiritual darkness of the world.) You can imagine the hatred that would allow these two bodies to lie in the street until the stench is unbearable. So great is the antagonism to their preaching of repentance that the whole earth will "rejoice over them, and make merry, and shall send gifts one to another, because these two prophets tormented them that dwelt on the earth." Verse 10. Every time a prophet of God preaches to people about their sins, there is a certain amount of resentment on the sinner's part. But just imagine the death of these two witnesses invoking rejoicing throughout the earth to such an extent that a holiday is proclaimed, and they that dwell on the earth send gifts to one another in exultation over the death of these two prophets.

RESURRECTION

The forces of Satan will not have long to glory in their deaths, however, for in 3½ days "the spirit of life from God entered into them, and they stood upon their feet, and great fear fell upon them who saw them." Verse 11. Before the very eyes of a multitude of witnesses, God will raise to life His two prophets and shall call them to come up to Him. They will ascend up to heaven in a cloud as their enemies behold them. Here is another great victory for God. So great is the impact of this resurrection to life that in the same hour as the two witnesses ascend into heaven, a great earthquake destroys a tenth of the city of Jerusalem and 7,000 men are swallowed up as those who remain give glory to the God of heaven. Such is the end of the second woe, but a third woe is coming quickly.

THE SEVENTH TRUMPET (11:15-19)

At verse 15 the narrative of future events again resumes and with the blowing of the seventh trumpet comes a dramatic announcement. "The kingdom of this world is become the kingdom of our Lord, and of his Christ, and he shall reign forever and ever." This is the beginning of the end and even though some additional events must transpire before the kingdom is established, nevertheless the announcement is made for victory is in the air. This will be the fulfillment of many Old Testament prophecies. Psalm 2:2; Dan. 2:44; Isa. 9:6-7.

Immediately the twenty-four elders fall down before God and worship Him for claiming what has been His all along. Verse 16.

In the midst of the elders' praise John sees the temple of God as the heavens open and in the temple is the ark of His covenant. Lightnings, voices, thunder, an earthquake and great hail are seen as well.

This event just precedes the final outpouring of judgment and as we have seen, the judgments are gaining in severity. Since the temple in Jerusalem has been defiled by the beast, it is not surprising to see a heavenly temple from which God rules in holiness. The presence of the ark of the covenant indicates that the judgments about to take place are based on the law and God always keeps His covenants. As God is faithful to us who will be raptured before this period of Tribulation, so too He will be faithful to those who trust Him during this hour of trial.

Bill 7-31-06 Read
Read next

*august 4-06*
august 4 06

THE WORLD AT WAR

Chapter 12

War is an ugly word. None of us even like to think of it
for we have experienced too much of it. Yet war seems to be
a fact of life because sin is a fact of life. Revelation chapter
12 is one of the most important chapters in the book, for it
describes the outbreak of war, past, present and future. This
war first takes place on earth, verses 1-6, then in heaven,
verses 7-12, and finally back on earth again, verses 13-17.
Let's look at the character of this war more closely.

THE WOMAN

Verse one indicates that there appears in heaven a great
"wonder" or "sign." You'll recall that Revelation is a book
that is sign-i-fied. Such is the case here. The great wonder or
sign that appears in heaven is a "woman clothed with the sun,
and the moon under her feet, and upon her head a crown of
twelve stars."

The imagery of this verse gives us a good clue to the
woman's identity. First, the figure of a woman is frequently
used as a symbol of religion. Jezebel represents paganism and
idolatrous worship. Rev. 2:20; I Kings 16:31. The Bride of
Christ represents the true Church. Rev. 19. So too the woman
here represents worship. Second, this woman is clothed with
the sun. The moon is under her feet. Her crown is made up of
twelve stars. There is only one place in the Bible where similar imagery is used. This is in the dream of Joseph where the
sun and moon and eleven other stars did obeisance to him.
Both Joseph and his father, Jacob, recognized the meaning of
this dream. Gen. 37:9-11. It referred to the nation Israel as
does the woman here in Revelation 12.

This woman, Israel, is pictured as being with child, crying, travailing in birth and being constantly in pain to be delivered. Rev. 12:2. Here is a perfect picture of the nation Israel from the call of Abraham to the birth of Christ. She was constantly expecting the birth of the Messiah, constantly in pain. There is no question but that the woman refers to Israel.

Bill 7-31-06

THE RED DRAGON

Verses three and four tell us of another wonder or sign in heaven. This time it is a great red dragon with seven heads, ten horns and seven crowns upon his heads. This dragon has a tail which drew a third of the stars of heaven with him casting them to the earth. The dragon is the arch-enemy of the woman and stands ready to devour her child as soon as it is born.

It certainly doesn't take much imagination to identify the dragon. This monster is none other than Satan. The stars which he drew from heaven and cast to the earth are the angels which fell with him when he attempted to usurp the throne of God. This open rebellion against God brought sin forth and caused a third of the angels to be cast out of God's presence. Jude 6; II Peter 2:4.

THE MALE CHILD

Verses five and six reveal another personality. The woman is pictured as bringing forth a male child **"who was to rule all nations with a rod of iron; and her child was caught up unto God, and to his throne."** Here the identification is obvious. This male child is Jesus Christ. Israel gave birth to the Messiah after travailing from the days of Abraham. At our Lord's birth the red dragon, Satan, had King Herod all ready to devour the Christ child but God providentially intervened. Matt. 2:13-18. The only person who is said to rule all nations with a rod of iron is Jesus Christ. Psalm 2:8-9; Rev. 19:15. And of course the only person ever caught up to God, to the throne of God, was our Lord. Luke 24:51; Acts 1:9-11. Hence, the male child of the woman Israel is Jesus Christ our Lord, the Messiah of Israel.

Bill 7-31-06

During Christ's earthly life, Satan did his best to war against Him and devour Him. But time and time again the war went badly for the red dragon. He was defeated at Bethlehem, at Calvary and finally at the Mount of Olives.

Between verses five and six is a prophetic gap. After Christ was caught up to heaven, the age of His Church was ushered in and Israel was set aside as a nation. That is why nothing is recorded here about Israel in the Church age. Verse six resumes the dealings of God with Israel and reveals what will become of this nation during the last half of Daniel's 70th week, the Tribulation. Since Satan has been totally unsuccessful in destroying the male child of the woman, he turns his attention to the woman herself. Satan's wrath is vented toward the nation Israel, especially during the final three years of Tribulation. Thus, Israel is forced to flee into the wilderness where God has prepared a place of shelter and safety for her. When Christ gave His great prophecy about the Great Tribulation, He warned, **"Then let them who are in Judaea flee into the mountains."** Matt. 24:16.

WILDERNESS HIDEAWAY

Perhaps we can identify this wilderness hideaway even further. The prophet Isaiah mentions the city of Sela in the wilderness of Moab as a place to hide the outcasts. "Let mine outcasts dwell with thee, Moab; be thou a covert to them from the face of the spoiler; for the extortioner is at an end, the spoiler ceaseth, the oppressors are consumed out of the land." Isa. 16:1-4. Sela is the Hebrew form of the Greek name Petra, meaning rock. Located some fifty miles south of the Dead Sea, the city of Petra was the capital of the ancient Edomite empire. Since it is situated in a fertile basin at an elevation of 2,700 feet above sea level and since it is entered only by a narrow twisting gorge whose walls rise a thousand feet higher, this spot seems to be the perfect hideaway for Israel. Here she will be protected for the last three and one-half years of intense persecution.

WAR IN HEAVEN

With verse seven the scene of war shifts from earth to heaven. Think of the consequences of the statement, **"And there was war in heaven."** The lines of battle are drawn: Michael and his angels versus the dragon and his angels. In Daniel 12:1 the archangel Michael is depicted as the special guardian of Israel. The red dragon is, of course, Satan who is mentioned specifically in verse nine. Here five individual titles are given this dragon. "Dragon" indicates his fierce nature, "serpent" his crafty nature, "devil" his accusing nature. "Satan" literally means adversary and "who deceiveth the whole world" gives us the number one activity of Satan.

The war in heaven, which means "the heavens" or the atmosphere, the air, appears to rage on for an extended period of time. Perhaps this great atmospheric battle takes place during the first three and one-half years of the Tribulation and may be instigated by the violation of the air space under Satan's control when the Lord Jesus raptures His Church. Eph. 2:2; I Thess. 4:17. When the dust settles not only could the dragon not prevail, verse eight, but a place is no longer found for him in the atmosphere and thus he is cast to the earth with his angels. Verse 9. With Satan and his demons cast to the ground, God reigns free and unincumbered in the three heavens. No more does Satan have access to God to accuse the brethren, as he did in the case of Job. Job 1. (H. A. Ironside used to say, "Satan is the accuser of the brethren; let's leave the dirty work to him!")

A SOLEMN WOE

However, having been cast out of the air means Satan can intensify his activity on the earth. A solemn woe is pronounced upon the inhabiters of the earth and the sea, for the devil is come down and is possessed with great wrath. The devil is aware "that he hath but a short time." Verse 12. This obviously is a reference to the fact that in three and one-half years, at the end of the Great Tribulation, Satan will be bound for one thousand years as Jesus Christ establishes His kingdom and reigns in righteousness on this earth. Being aware of this we can expect the activity of Satan to dramatically increase after he is cast to the earth.

But the brethren living at that time can still have victory over the red dragon. They have it the same way we have been victorious over him. **"And they overcame him by the blood of the Lamb, and by the word of their testimony; and they loved not their lives unto the death."** Verse 11. The blood of Jesus Christ not only cleanses us from sin, it defeats Satan in the process, as it will do for these Tribulation saints.

SATAN'S ANTI-SEMITISM

Beginning with verse 13, the war with Satan returns to earth. Thwarted in his last attempt on earth to destroy Jesus Christ, the male child of the woman, and defeated in the heavens, Satan now turns his attention to the woman as was previously mentioned in verse six. The anti-Semitism of Satan is the most intense ever, for Israel is symbolic of the worship of God which Satan hates. As Israel rapidly flees to the wilderness, Satan causes a great flood to go forth in an attempt to destroy her. But in the providence of God, even the earth aids the woman and the great flood is swallowed up by the earth. The dragon is now exceedingly wroth with Israel and takes his anger out on those who do not flee to the wilderness. Jews who turn to Christ, "who keep the commandments of God, and have the testimony of Jesus Christ" (verse 17) will be the special target of Satan's wrath as he unleashes an attack on the Jews which is unparalleled in history.

As you have now realized, chapter 12 is an inset into the narrative of future events. Its lines of truth stretch both back to the days of Christ and forward to the end of the Great Tribulation. It gives us a comprehensive view of the deceptive activity of Satan. Each of us should beware even now for Satan is bent on destroying whoever stands for God in this world. In this Church age, we are his target. Let's "be sober, be vigilant, because your adversary, the devil, like a roaring lion walketh about, seeking whom he may devour." I Peter 5:8.

7-31-06 Bill

Here next. —Bill

THE RISE OF ANTICHRIST

Chapter 13

The career of Satan has been a long and infamous one. But from the very moment he lifted his head in pride against God, his goal has always been the same. Lucifer wants to be God. He was not happy with being a beautiful angel. His jealousy of God turned ambition into rebellion. He said, "I will ascend into heaven, I will exalt my throne above the stars of God; I will sit also upon the mount of the congregation, in the sides of the north, I will ascend above the heights of the clouds, I will be like the Most High." Isa. 14:13-14.

THE TRINITY OF EVIL

Since Satan's ambition to be God is impossible, he attempts the next best thing. Satan imitates God and by doing so, deceives people into believing he is God. This is what he did through the Pharaoh's magicians. This is what he is doing today in leading so many unsuspecting people into joining satanic cults and worshiping demons.

But it is during the dark days of the Tribulation that Satan will be most successful in imitating God. In fact, during this period of judgment upon the earth, Satan will produce a counterfeit trinity. This evil trinity will be composed of Satan, the Antichrist and the False Prophet.

THE FALSE FATHER

Satan is the opposite of God the Father and occupies His position in the evil trinity. Revelation 12:9 reveals that Satan is a great fiery monster, brilliant, formidable, a great dragon. Ezek. 28:12. He is that old serpent who introduced sin into the world. Gen. 3:1. He is a deceiver, slanderer, accuser of the brethren. He is the Devil. Rev. 12:10. He is

Satan, the adversary of God and His people. Zech. 3:1. And by feigning the trinity of the most holy God, Satan deceives the whole world, being a liar right from the beginning and the father of the lie. John 8:44. Through deception, trickery and just plain lying, Satan makes himself out to be God the Father.

THE FALSE SON

In Revelation 13 the other two members of this false trinity are introduced. As Satan is the false Father, verse one depicts the rise of the false Son, the false Christ. "And I stood upon the sand of the sea, and saw a beast rise up out of the sea, having seven heads and ten horns, and upon his horns ten crowns, and upon his heads the name of blasphemy." This beast is a man (who very well could be alive today) for he is expressly called thus in verse 18 of this chapter and is treated as a man in other Scriptures. Dan. 7:8; II Thess. 2:3-4; Rev. 19:19-20. He is said to arise "out of the sea," an expression which signifies the Gentile nations. This false Christ or Antichrist is described as a king. Rev. 17:10-11.

A REVIVED EMPIRE

However, the beast is more than a man, more than a king. He is also a kingdom. The seven heads and ten horns with ten crowns speak of a kingdom. The ten horns are identified as ten kings in 17:12; yet they are united in one beast. In other words, the Antichrist represents a confederation of ten kingdoms or countries. Since a similar description is given in Daniel 7:7-8, this beast's kingdom must be the revived Roman Empire. Ancient Rome was built on seven hills, represented by the seven heads — there is no better way to signify an empire than with the symbol of its king. Dan. 7:7, 17, 23.

Further confirmation that the Antichrist's kingdom is the revival of the Roman Empire is seen in verse two. John records, "And the beast which I saw was like a leopard, and his feet were like the feet of a bear, and his mouth like the mouth of a lion; and the dragon gave him his power, and his throne, and great authority." The description of the false

Christ as "like a leopard, and his feet were like the feet of a bear, and his mouth like the mouth of a lion" is very meaningful. In Daniel two and again in the vision of Daniel seven, the prophet Daniel saw four great successive world empires: the lion, referring to Babylon; the bear, referring to Medo-Persia; and the leopard, referring to the Grecian Empire. The last great empire took the dominant elements and characteristics of the first three and combined them in itself. The qualities of strength, brutality and swiftness were all present in the final empire, which was Rome.

A WOUNDED HEAD

So closely identified are the ruler and his kingdom that verse three speaks of **"one of his heads as though it were wounded to death; and his deadly wound was healed, and all the world wondered after the beast."** The meaning could be twofold. In order to deceive the world into believing that he is Christ, the Antichrist may receive a death blow. Since it is questionable whether Satan can actually raise a person from the dead, the Antichrist probably only pretends to be dead and then rises again deceiving people into believing that he is an authentic saviour. But the primary meaning here is that of the kingdom, not the king. This verse signifies that the Roman Empire, although apparently dead, will be revived in order to provide the Antichrist with a base of operations, a kingdom, a throne and great authority. Verse 2.

AMBITION FULFILLED

At this eventful point in history, Satan will receive something he has always wanted. Through his man, the Antichrist, whom he makes the ruler of the world, Satan will receive worship and praise. Verse 4 indicates, **"And they worshiped the dragon who gave power unto the beast; and they worshiped the beast, saying, Who is like the beast? Who is able to make war with him?"** Satan takes credit for the miraculous phenomena which take place during the Tribulation. Unable to explain it, the people of the earth believe Satan's lie given to the world through the Antichrist and fall down and worship them both. They cry, "Who is like the beast?

Who is able to make war with him?" The unique character of
the beast and his might make the people stand in awe. These
same individuals were confronted with the unique character
of Jesus Christ and His might before the rapture and yet they
did not believe. Now they believe without reservation in
Satan and Antichrist.

However, not everyone will worship the imposter Christ.
Verse eight indicates, **"And all that dwell upon the earth shall
worship him, whose names are not written in the book of life
of the Lamb slain from the foundation of the world."** The
saved of this period will stand true to God the Father and
God the Son even though it means death for many of them.

SATANIC MOUTHPIECE

In the trinity of God, Jesus Christ came to earth and
spoke the words of God, revealing the thoughts and mind of
God. So too the second person of this evil trinity will be the
spokesman for Satan. Verse five reads, "And there was given
unto him a mouth speaking great things . . . " This indicates
that Antichrist's message is not his own but rather that of
Satan. Unlike the true Christ, who spoke in praise of God the
Father and provided the basis for peace with God by shed-
ding His own precious blood, the activities of the false Christ
will be greatly different. He will speak blasphemies and en-
gage in war.

Verse six indicates that this man "opened his mouth in
blasphemy against God, to blaspheme his name, and his taber-
nacle, and them that dwell in heaven." Did you notice what
Antichrist will blaspheme? His main target is God but he also
pours out venomous blasphemy against the house of God and
the children of God. Beloved, we won't even be safe from
slander when we get to heaven. However, these satanic blasphemies against us can't harm us, safe in the arms of Jesus.

SAINTS MARTYRED

Satan continues to use Antichrist by giving him the
power or civil authority to make war against the saints and to

On to the next Page

overcome them. Those who stand true for the faith during the Great Tribulation will have no civil liberties and will be viciously attacked by the Antichrist and killed in the name of the empire. During this period, born-again believers will be persecuted and murdered much as they were in the second century under the original Roman Empire.

WORLD RULER

That Antichrist is a world ruler is evident from the fact that his power was over all kindreds, peoples, tongues and nations. Undoubtedly he will be gathering power throughout the first half of the Tribulation but will not receive world rulership until he breaks the covenant of peace with Israel. Dan. 9:27. Then, acting as the tool of Satan, the beast will wage all-out war against Israel and the saints of God throughout the entire globe and will overcome them. Dan. 7:25; 9:27; 12:10; Rev. 7:9-17. In the will of the Father, many believers will perish as martyrs while others are preserved alive in spite of all the blasphemy and war of the impostor Christ.

This will be the heyday of Satan. He will receive praise and worship. He will envision himself as God. The second person of this evil trinity will speak forcefully for Satan and the majority of the world will fall in line against God and those who represent Him on the earth. The dream of world conquest by the Babylonian, Medo-Persian, Grecian and Roman empires will now for the first time be realized completely under the reign of Satan and Antichrist. A counterfeit millennium will be instituted. All of this is permitted by God in a final display of Satan's evil. The picture is dark indeed, but beloved, if we look a little farther down the road John writes, "And I saw, as it were, a sea of glass mingled with fire, and them that had gotten the victory over the beast, and over his image, and over his mark, and over the number of his name, standing on the sea of glass, having the harps of God." Rev. 15:2. Friends, God will permit Satan to force his counterfeit trinity on this earth for awhile, but He won't permit it forever. As always in history, God's children are promised and assured of ultimate victory.

Read next 8-4-06

THE RISE OF THE FALSE PROPHET

Chapters 13-14

The last half of Revelation 13 records John's vision of the third member of the trinity of evil. The dragon (Satan) is the antithesis of God the Father. The first beast, the beast out of the sea (Antichrist), is the antithesis of God the Son. Now another beast arises (the False Prophet) and is the antithesis of God the Spirit. As the heavenly trinity is made up of three persons, Father, Son and Holy Spirit, this counterfeit, hellish trinity is made up of three persons: Satan, Antichrist and False Prophet.

The appearance of the second beast out of the earth is far less pretentious than the first. Instead of seven heads and ten horns with ten crowns, this beast has only two horns. There are a number of ways in which this impostor poses as the counterpart of the Spirit of God.

THE FALSE SPIRIT

First, note that he appears on the scene "like a lamb." Rev. 13:11. He is not a lamb but appears like a lamb. If he was a lamb, we would think him an impostor of Jesus Christ. But since he appears like a lamb, he imitates the Spirit of Christ. As the Holy Spirit produces Christ-likeness in us, this False Prophet will produce Antichrist-likeness in the lives of those who worship the beast.

Second, note in verse 12 that "he exerciseth all the power of the first beast before him . . ." You will recall our Lord's command, "And, behold, I send the promise of my Father upon you; but tarry ye in the city of Jerusalem, until ye be endued with power from on high." Luke 24:49. That promised power came in the person of the Holy Spirit. "But

— 47 — Bill / 8.4.06

Read on →

ye shall receive power, after the Holy Spirit is come upon you." Acts 1:8. Whenever the Spirit of God is mentioned in Scripture, He is always associated with power. During the Great Tribulation the False Prophet imitates the Holy Spirit by exerting the power of Antichrist.

Third, verse 12 continues, **"and causeth the earth and them who dwell on it to worship the first beast, whose deadly wound was healed."** The aim of the second beast is to promote the worship of Antichrist. At no time in his career does he promote himself. This is true with the Holy Spirit. He causes men and women to worship Jesus Christ. He does not attract attention to Himself but always points to Christ. Those who currently place an overemphasis on the baptism and work of the Spirit of God defeat His purpose. Jesus Christ came to give life; the Holy Spirit is come to comfort and point men to Christ. Likewise, the False Prophet does not seek attention but seeks to divert attention to the Antichrist.

Fourth, we learn from verse 13 that the second beast **"doeth great wonders, so that he maketh fire come down from heaven on the earth in the sight of men."** Again and again the Holy Spirit is associated with fire. When the Spirit came upon the Church at Pentecost "there appeared unto them cloven tongues as of fire, and it sat upon each of them." Acts 2:2-3.

Here, perhaps, the False Prophet is imitating more than the Holy Spirit at Pentecost. The two witnesses were divinely commissioned and empowered by God and had the ability to perform miracles including the issue of fire out of their mouths devouring their enemies. Not to be outdone by his religious adversaries, the False Prophet also performs wonders or signs including the calling forth of fire. All of this is a part of the strong delusion mentioned in II Thessalonians 2:11.

The final way in which the False Prophet imitates the Holy Spirit is found in verse 15. **"And he hath power to give** life unto the image of the beast, that the image of the beast should both speak, and cause that as many as would not worship the image of the beast should be killed." As Satan's religious leader during the Tribulation, the False Prophet will issue an ecclesiastical edict commanding that an image of the beast be made. This will become the focal point of their false system of worship.

The expression "he had power to give life unto the image of the beast" is properly translated "it was given to him to give spirit to the image of the beast." The Greek word here is *pneuma* which means "spirit" or "breath" and is quite different from the word meaning "life." The magical power that Antichrist gives the False Prophet is not to give life to an inanimate object but to give the "appearance" of life. The satanic image of the beast will be given the appearance of breathing and moving, either mechanically like a robot or by being indwelt with one of Satan's demons. Whatever the case, the masses will believe it is alive and will worship it.

THE MARK OF THE BEAST

The last three verses of this chapter inform us of the universal, religious influence of this counterfeit holy spirit. "And he causeth all, both small and great, rich and poor, free and enslaved, to receive a mark in their right hand, or in their foreheads." This mark is placed in the most conspicuous places of the body — the forehead or right hand. Again you can see imitation. As the Holy Spirit is the sealer of the redeemed (Eph. 1:13; 4:30) and as 144,000 are sealed out of Israel unto God, now we see the false spirit placing a mark or seal on his followers.

The reason for the mark on the forehead or right hand is explained in verse 17. "And that no man might buy or sell, except he that had the mark, or the name of the beast, or the number of his name." Some time ago my daughter was invited to a birthday party held at a kiddieland amusement park. When each of the children arrived, they were stamped on the back of the right hand with a rubber stamp. Without that stamp they could not ride any of the rides. How that made me think of the False Prophet and the terrible days of the Great Tribulation. Without the mark of the beast no one will be able to buy, sell or trade. Life will come to a grinding halt without that mark. The False Prophet will ration commodities only to those who have it.

666

What that mark is seems to be identified in verse 18. "Here is wisdom. Let him that hath understanding count the number of the beast; for it is the number of a man; and his number is six hundred threescore and six." The number of the beast is simply the number of man. Six is man's number as evidenced by the fact that he was created on the sixth day, he was to work six days, etc. The image of Nebuchadnezzar was sixty cubits high and six cubits broad.

Opposed to this is seven, the number of God. His creative activity was completed and He rested on the 7th day. Seven is the number of both completion and perfection. This entire book of Revelation is built around the number seven. We are studying seven groups of seven things in each group. We note: seven churches, seven seals, seven trumpets, seven personalities, seven vials, seven dooms, and seven new things. This is God's perfect way of completing His revelation to man.

With this in mind, it is easy to understand that the number assigned to the unholy trinity is 666, less than perfect but a multiple of man at his best, the highest Satan can attain. Hence, this is an appropriate mark for the trinity of evil; Satan, Antichrist and the False Prophet. In those dark days of deception, Satan is the unseen ruler, the Antichrist the world political ruler and the False Prophet the world religious ruler. Together they will lie, murder, ration and force their way into rulership of the entire world.

THE LAMB ON MT. ZION

In the midst of this dismal revelation about the last days of the Tribulation, John is given another parenthetic vision recorded in chapter 14. As if to encourage him as he wrote, God allows John to see the Lamb, Christ Jesus, standing on Mount Zion with the 144,000. They are singing a new song before the throne, perhaps one they have been taught by the 24 elders. Can't you almost hear them sing, "Redeemed how I love to proclaim it! Redeemed by the blood of the Lamb; Redeemed thro' His infinite mercy, His child, and forever, I am."

John also sees an "angel fly in the midst of heaven, having the everlasting gospel to preach . . ." Verse 6. Beloved, whether in the Old Testament, New Testament, twentieth century, or Tribulation, there is but one Gospel of salvation. It is the everlasting Gospel of God's love and Christ's atonement.

In verse eight John views another angel predicting the fall of Babylon quickly followed by a third angel who speaks with a loud voice declaring the doom of those who bow down and worship the beast. Verses 9-12. Suddenly a voice from heaven instructs John to write these words, "Blessed are the dead who die in the Lord from henceforth. Yea, saith the Spirit, that they may rest from their labors, and their works do follow them." Verse 13.

VISION OF ARMAGEDDON

Finally, in this parenthetic chapter just before the most severe judgment of the seven bowls, John's heart is encouraged by getting just a glimpse of the battle of Armageddon where the great winepress of God's wrath will pour forth tremendous judgment. Isn't it grand how God knows just when we need encouragement. Having received the vision of the seven trumpets and about to embark on the vision of the seven vials, what better encouragement could God give than to show the Apostle John a glimpse of the end and the ultimate victory of God.

This same function the Book of Revelation performs for us. Bogged down in the trials and troubles of life, there is a great uplift and encouragement to be had in reading the Revelation for it shows us that the victory is ultimately God's. Perhaps this is the blessing that is promised to everyone who reads or hears the words of this prophecy. Rev. 1:3.

THE SEVEN BOWL JUDGMENTS

Chapters 15-16

As you read chapters 15 and 16 of Revelation you get the definite impression that the climax is coming. There is an air of expectancy, of finality. Each of the judgments through the seven seals and seven trumpets are increasingly more severe. But now God's judgment upon this wicked earth is rising to a crescendo. John is permitted yet another vision, this one great and marvelous, and views seven angels bearing the seven last plagues. Judgment is about to be poured out as history has never seen it before.

Let's notice three important features in Revelation 15 and 16. They are: God's righteousness, God's wrath, and man's response. That God is righteous and holy in His dealings with mankind is firmly established in Scripture. Gen. 18:25; Deut. 32:4; Psalm 7:9-12; Rom. 2:5. Here again we have affirmation of His righteousness. John envisions those who "had gotten the victory over the beast, and over his image, and over his mark, and over the number of his name, standing on the sea of glass, having the harps of God." Rev. 15:2. These are the martyred dead who did not yield to the beast's demand for blasphemy and thus are pictured as the triumphant.

They sing the song of Moses and the song of the Lamb and exclaim, "Great and marvelous are thy works, Lord God Almighty, just and true are thy ways, thou King of saints. Who shall not fear thee, O Lord, and glorify thy name? For thou only art holy; for all nations shall come and worship before thee; for thy judgments are made manifest." Verses 3-4.

You may ask, if God is so righteous, why does He suddenly appear so avengeful? Why does He allow such tremendous wrath to pour out on the earth? The answer is simple. Today we view God as He deals in mercy and grace. This is the dispensation of grace. However, God has promised judgment and payment for sin and He wouldn't be just and righteous unless He fulfilled that promise. When the age of grace is passed, the age of judgment is ushered in. In Revelation 4-19 we are viewing God at work in the day of righteous judgment.

Verses five through eight of this chapter give clear indication that God is just in delivering judgment on the earth. The picture of the heavenly temple containing the ark of the covenant makes it evident that God is not dealing in grace but according to divine law. Verse 5. Those who have broken God's law are now judged by it.

His agents of judgment are seven angels, clothed in pure and white linen with golden belts. They originate in the heavenly temple and as they leave to bring judgment each one receives a golden vial or bowl filled to the brim with the wrath of God. Verses 6-7. Throughout the entire span of the seven bowl judgments the heavenly throneroom is filled with smoke from the glory and power of God. Verse 8. All of this suggests the sovereignty of God and His righteousness and justice in bringing judgment to sinful man.

With the beginning of chapter 16 we notice the second important feature of these chapters. This is God's wrath. John hears the voice of God say to the seven angels, **"Go your ways, and pour out the bowls of the wrath of God upon the earth."** Apparently these seven judgments occur in rapid succession. Immediately the first leaves the heavens and proceeds to dump the wrath of God out of his bowl.

THE FIRST BOWL (16:2)

When the first bowl is emptied "there fell a foul and painful sore upon the men who had the mark of the beast, and upon them who worshiped his image." This judgment is an evil or malignant sore, rotten and incurable, similar to the boils inflicted on the Egyptians in Exodus 9:9-11. The extent of this affliction is limited to those who have received the mark of the beast or have bowed to his image. Those few who remain true to God are exempt. Ex. 9:8-12.

THE SECOND BOWL (16:3)

"And the second angel poured out his bowl upon the sea, and it became like the blood of a dead man; and every living soul died in the sea." The analogy here is to the first of the ten plagues of Egypt (Ex. 7:20-25) in which the Nile turned to blood, killing all the fish and making the water unfit to drink. The sea becoming as the blood of a dead man is a vivid picture of a man wallowing in his own blood. One-third of the sea animals died under the second trumpet. Rev. 8:9. Now the destruction is total and marine bodies as well as men will be wallowing in the blood of the sea.

THE THIRD BOWL (16:4-7)

The third bowl of God's wrath is poured out upon the rivers and fountains of waters and they too become blood. Rivers of blood pour from the ground adding to the problem of obtaining fresh drinking water.

Here the angel adds a brief footnote indicating God is righteous in causing the water and sources of water to become blood. This is the unchanging law of divine retribution. Throughout the Tribulation period the forces of Satan have been spilling the blood of the saints as if it were water. Now, because of these acts of infamy, they are getting their fill of blood. The angel says, "Thou art righteous, O Lord, who art, and wast, and shalt be, because thou hast judged thus. For they have shed the blood of saints and prophets, and thou hast given them blood to drink; for they are worthy." Verses 5-6.

Again, bear in mind that God is now dealing not in grace but in judgment. These bloodthirsty inhabitants of the earth are getting just what they deserve, for they have consistently spilled the blood of the saints. As the Tribulation draws to a close, God deals in harsh justice.

THE FOURTH BOWL (16:8-9)

"And the fourth angel poured out his bowl upon the sun, and power was given unto him (the sun) to scorch men with fire. And men were scorched with great heat . . ." When the temperature climbs into the 90's today we glibly exclaim, "It's a real scorcher" and turn on the fan or air conditioner. However, we know nothing of the scorching heat that will one day torture the ungodly inhabitants of this earth. With the shortages of energy due to rationing and the great judgments of God, there will be no air conditioners or any other forms of relief from the scorching heat of the sun which has been intensified by God.

THE FIFTH BOWL (16:10-11)

The fifth plague of judgment attacks the very throne of the beast. As in the fifth trumpet judgment and in the ninth plague of Egypt (Ex. 10:21-23) there is darkness over the earth. It will be pitch black. So dark you can feel it. But this is only part of this bowl's judgment.

The sores inflicted upon the worshipers of the beast are still very painful and the beast will not be able to work his magic in curing them. Terrible pain results in this intense darkness. So unbearable is the pain that men will gnaw their tongues in severe agony. Apparently the darkness aggravates the pain and the results of judgment are compounded.

THE SIXTH BOWL (16:12)

"And the sixth angel poured out his bowl upon the great river, Euphrates, and its water was dried up, that the way of the kings of the east might be prepared." The Great Tribulation is fast coming to a climactic end. With the emptying of the sixth bowl the great river Euphrates is dried up. Flowing some 1,800 miles from the mountains to the Persian Gulf, it was too deep to ford and too long to go around.

Thus, with the sixth bowl of God's wrath emptied, the Euphrates ceases to be a barrier and opens the way for the kings of the east to march into the battle of Armageddon. Verses 13-16 actually give parenthetic information about this great battle. That's how closely tied the sixth and seventh bowls of wrath are to the triumph of God's judgment at Armageddon.

THE SEVENTH BOWL (16:17-21)

With the emptying of the seventh bowl comes the cry from the heavenly throne, "It is done." Judgment is soon to be completed. With this cry are the accompanying signs of voices, thunders, lightnings, a great earthquake (the likes of which man has never seen before). Jerusalem is upended and divided into three parts, Babylon is destroyed, islands of the sea disappear, mountains vanish and hail the size of a talent falls out of heaven. Friends, today we talk about hail the size of a golf ball. But when God's righteous judgment is poured out, the hail will weigh nearly 125 pounds. You can imagine the destruction.

We have seen God's righteousness in judgment and His wrath. But what is man's response? Does he fall on his knees and repent for worshiping the beast? Not at all. In the final illustration of the hardness of man's heart, no one repents or gives glory to God. Instead, they "blasphemed the name of God," verse nine, and "blasphemed the God of heaven because of their pains and their sores, and repented not of their deeds." Verse 11. "Men blasphemed God because of the plague of the hail, for the plague was exceedingly great." Verse 21. Even in judgment, when the righteousness of God is fully revealed through His wrath on sin, men and women will continue to harden their hearts, blaspheme His holy name, and choose to worship sin and the beast.

Friends, the wrath of God is coming on this earth. Even though we are living in the age of grace, in order to be forgiven of our sins by God, we must do the same thing that is necessary for those in the awful day of God's wrath. We must repent of our sin against God. We must cease blaspheming His holy name. We must not worship anyone or anything other than Him. We must be saved by the blood of Jesus Christ.

If you do not receive Jesus as Saviour now, while God is dealing in grace, you will surely face the wrath of God in judgment. The choice is yours. View the Tribulation from heaven in the company of Christ and His Church or endure it on earth in the torment of the seven bowls of God. Thank God for the opportunity to receive Jesus Christ by faith today.

ECCLESIASTICAL BABYLON

Chapter 17

Bill

8 aug — 06 start Tonight

By now you have become aware that the revelation received by John deals with different events which do not always proceed in chronological order. Occasionally John is drawn aside to receive additional information about something previously introduced but now more fully explained. On these occasions a chapter or two is inset into the narrative. Such is the case with chapters 17 and 18.

RELIGION AND POLITICS

In Revelation 14:8 the destruction of Babylon is foretold. Now John is given greater detail about its fall. Chapters 17 and 18 deal with the destruction of Babylon which represents religion and government in the end of the age. Revelation 17 records the destruction of ecclesiastical Babylon and Revelation 18 records the destruction of political Babylon.

These two events, however, do not take place at the same time. The destruction of Babylon, as representing the false religion of the future world church, chapter 17, best fits into the time period of the first 3½ years of Tribulation. When Christ raptures His Church and we go to live forever with Him, it doesn't mean the end of religion. Many churches and religious orders will function with "business as usual" for the Lord Jesus Christ is not a part of them even today. When as born-again believers we are taken to heaven, these religions will continue to thrive and Satan will even permit them to grow. The devil will use false religion for his own evil purposes until he no longer needs it. With the rise of the Antichrist, in the middle of the Tribulation, religious activity of all forms, except that instituted by this beast, will cease and the great ecclesiastical Babylon will be overthrown. This event is described in Revelation 17.

Read on

8-13-06

Bill

THE GREAT HARLOT

Verse one of the chapter says, "And there came one of the seven angels who had the seven bowls, and talked with me, saying unto me, Come here; I will show unto thee the judgment of the great harlot that sitteth upon many waters." We are immediately faced with the problem of identifying this great whore or harlot that is about to be judged. Verse five indicates that "upon her forehead was a name written, MYSTERY, BABYLON THE GREAT, THE MOTHER OF HARLOTS AND ABOMINATIONS OF THE EARTH." Hence, Scripture tells us that this harlot is Babylon the Great.

The matter of identifying this great city is a subject of much debate. There are many good Bible scholars who believe that this refers to the once great capital of the Babylonian Empire, now lying in ruins. They maintain that the city will be one day rebuilt and become both the religious and commercial center of the world. Jer. 50-51. However, this may not be the case. Babylon is frequently used in Scripture to refer to a system of idolatrous religion. It is important to bear in mind that in Revelation, Babylon refers to both a city and a religious system, just as Wall Street refers to both a street and a system of free economy. It is highly likely that this Babylon represents another city and religious system which displays the characteristics of the once evil Babylon.

Historical Babylon began in Genesis 10 and 11 when Nimrod, the fierce hunter and rebel against God, built a city and the people built the Tower of Babel in an attempt to reach heaven. From that time on Babylon became a symbol for a counterfeit or false religion and is actually the mother of all other religious heresies. Let me share with you the religion of ancient Babylon.

BABYLONIAN MYSTERY RELIGION

Nimrod's wife, Semiramis, founded the Babylonian mystery religion. (Remember, the name of the great harlot in Revelation is MYSTERY, BABYLON THE GREAT.) Semiramis knew God's promise to Eve that one day He would bring forth of her seed One who would bruise the head of Satan and give deliverance and redemption to mankind. Gen. 3:15. Aware of this, Nimrod's wife shrewdly connived a religion on the basis of that promise. She gave birth to a son whom she claimed was miraculously conceived without a human father. Soon images were made of Semiramis and her baby which became a central part of her idolatrous system of worship. The son, whose name was Tammuz, was worshipped as the saviour and redeemer of men, but it was Semiramis who was the real object of worship. She became known as the "queen of heaven" and demanded that little round cakes be offered in her honor. Later Jeremiah condemned the heathen practices of making cakes for the "queen of heaven" (Jer. 7:18) and offering incense to the "queen of heaven" (Jer. 44:17-19,25).

But Semiramis did not stop there. She introduced a doctrine of purging or purifying sin after death. In this mysterious Babylonian religion, salvation was obtained by countless sacraments, special feasts, rites and ceremonies. These included the Babylonian priests sprinkling holy water on the heads of all those who entered the pagan temples. Also, Semiramis established an order of virgins who wore long flowing robes and renounced all claims to ordinary life, liberty and the pursuit of happiness. They dedicated themselves exclusively to God and the service of the temple.

The wicked wife of Nimrod instituted the festival of Ishtar which was a period of weeping and mourning for Tammuz, because tradition says he was out hunting one day and was slain by a wild boar. Semiramis is then supposed to have wept for forty days and received her son back to life again. Ezekiel 8:14 records the protest of God's prophet over this pagan practice.

The false religion of ancient Babylon soon spread to other parts of the world under different names. Always the system of belief was the same, just the names were changed. Idols to the mother and child soon sprang up all over the world. In Egypt the mother was Isis, the son Horus. In Greece the mother was Aphrodite, the son Cupid. You don't have to look far to find a religious system containing these features today.

ROMAN CATHOLIC CHURCH

The religious system of ecclesiastical Babylon is described in Revelation 17 as a harlot sitting on many waters. Verse 15 interprets the waters as "peoples, and multitudes, and nations, and tongues." She is portrayed as committing spiritual fornication with the inhabitants of the earth. We have already pointed out that in the Book of Revelation the figure of a woman symbolizes religion. Jezebel represents the pagan idolatry of the past (2:20), the sun-clothed woman represents Israel (12:1), the Bride of Christ represents the true Church (21:9) and here we have the great harlot representing the false church, the modern-day descendant of the mystery religion of Semiramis. The woman is arrayed in purple and scarlet, bedecked with gold and precious stones and pearls. Rev. 17:4. That the woman is sitting upon seven mountains, which usually refers to the city of Rome, and with the great similarities between it and the religion of ancient Babylon, it is difficult to escape the conclusion that this woman refers to the Roman Catholic Church.

However, even though the Roman Church may be the basis for ecclesiastical Babylon, there are certainly Protestant churches and other churches of all religions involved here. This false system of worship described as the great harlot will include many groups as well as the mother church. This is the ecumenical movement at its height. Here we see one world church, based in Rome (religious Babylon) and practicing a system of worship which began back in ancient Babylon with the wicked wife of Nimrod. Friends, the one world church movement is part of the program of Antichrist. Ecclesiastical Babylon symbolizes apostate religion, religion without the power or presence of the Holy Spirit.

Read this ↗ Paragraph good

ECUMENICALISM DESTROYED

This composite, apostate church will make political alliances with the nation in order to gain power. The fact that she rules over "peoples, multitudes, and nations, and tongues" is proof positive that this will indeed be a politically-minded ecumenical church. But what will be the future of this ecclesiastical Babylon, this world-wide idolatrous church? Notice verse 16. "And the ten horns which thou sawest upon the beast, these shall hate the harlot, and shall make her desolate and naked, and shall eat her flesh, and burn her with fire." By comparing other Scriptures we may place this annihilation of the one world church midway through the seven years of Tribulation. During the first half of this period religious freedom is extended to all. All the religions of the world, apart from those who remain true to Christ, will gather in one great world church. The climax of this gathering is seen in the pomp and ceremony of the harlot riding on the beast.

However, with the revival of the Roman Empire, the beast no longer needs the church to gain power. Thus he destroys the world church and substitutes the worship of himself. The false system of religion called Babylon, the harlot, will vanish and the beast will be unchallenged as world leader and his False Prophet as world religious leader. Using the power he has over the ten horns, the league of ten nations, Antichrist will utterly destroy all forms of religion, even the apostate Christianity known as ecclesiastical Babylon centered in the Church of Rome.

All of this is in the will and plan of God. Rev. 17:17. God has never been pleased with systems of worship which do not give Him His rightful place and counterfeit or divert the honor that is due only to God. Thus, the ecumenical movement and those Roman Catholic, Protestant and other churches so intimately involved in it are doomed to be destroyed by the Antichrist after he has used them to gain world rulership.

Read this

Friend, listen to me. Only Jesus Christ can save you from sin. No church or religious system can. The present-day heir of Semiramis' mystery religion, which is called Babylon the harlot, is the united world church which so many are calling for today. It is doomed to death after it has been duped and used by the Antichrist. Do not become involved with it. Rather, become involved with Jesus Christ who came to seek and to save that which was lost. Luke 19:10. He alone can save you and remove you from this earth before the terrible events of the Tribulation begin. Trust only in Him today.

Read this Paragraph
all

— 64 —

POLITICAL BABYLON

Chapter 18

The preceding chapter recorded the fall of the great harlot, Babylon the Great. It is likely that this event takes place in the middle of the Tribulation for the fall of the harlot is the destruction of the false system of religion which Satan has supported through the centuries. It is the destruction of the ecumenical church, the one world church, after Antichrist no longer needs it.

In chapter 18 we have more information about the fall of Babylon. This time it is the fall of political or governmental Babylon. The difference in emphasis between the two chapters is this. In chapter 17 it was the beast and his ten-nation confederacy who destroyed religious Babylon. In chapter 18 political Babylon is destroyed by God Himself in preparation for the coming of the KING OF KINGS AND LORD OF LORDS.

ECCLESIASTICAL BABYLON FORNICATES

Verses one through three read, "And after these things I saw another angel come down from heaven, having great power, and the earth was made bright with his glory. And he cried mightily with a strong voice, saying, Babylon the great is fallen, is fallen, and is become the habitation of demons, and the hold of every foul spirit, and a cage of every unclean and hateful bird. For all nations have drunk of the wine of the wrath of her fornication, and the kings of the earth have committed fornication with her, and the merchants of the earth are grown rich through the abundance of her delicacies." The great harlot is fallen. Babylon as a system of religion is demonic. She is unfaithful to God and has spiritually fornicated with the nations of the world, soiling the message of true religion. Babylon is intoxicating and drags down with her the nations who align themselves with this false church. They have an easy form of religion with the harlot; a few dollars can make the church look the other way. No wonder they weep over her destruction.

It is evident that with the corruption of this end-time system of religion many people will become wealthy. There is much business transacted in the church of the great harlot. She has accumulated great wealth and is a powerful force in business. We see this in the mother church of Rome today.

Thus, John is permitted to hear another voice from heaven saying, "Come out of her, my people, that ye be not partakers of her sins, and that ye receive not of her plagues." Verse 4. Beloved, isn't that reminiscent of God's call to Lot begging him to leave worldly Sodom before total judgment? Gen. 19:15-22. Here men and women of the Tribulation period are urged by God to come out of ecclesiastical Babylon just as the children of Israel were urged to come out of ancient Babylon. Jer. 51:45. And why? Because by separating themselves from this apostate form of Christianity they will not partake of her sin and will not have the plagues inflicted on them that are certain to afflict ecclesiastical Babylon. Verses 6 and 8.

POLITICAL BABYLON TIED TO THE CHURCH

Political and economic Babylon now comes into view. With the destruction of the false church comes the collapse of the financial association between the ecumenical church and the nations. Thus, verse 9 records, "And the kings of the earth, who have committed fornication and lived luxuriously with her, shall bewail her, and lament for her, when they shall see the smoke of her burning." Now the economic and political city symbolized by Babylon is destroyed. The kings of the earth lament because of the collapse of the false church. Without her there is no means of supporting their governments for they are built on an alliance with the false religious system. Hence the confederation of nations and their governments also collapse.

It seems likely, since Rome is the seat of the apostate church and is described by the seven mountains of Revelation 17:9, that it is both the religious and political city that falls. The city which thrived on false religion and financially benefited from it will now economically collapse. The burning of the city is a symbol of the fall of its political and economic might, and the kings of the earth marvel at the destruction of the powerful capital of Antichrist's world empire.

It is almost unbelievable the effect that the collapse of religious and political Babylon will have on the people of the earth. Not only do the kings or heads of state bemoan her fate, but commercial officials do as well. Their source of gain is suddenly gone. Verse 11 relates to us, "And the merchants of the earth shall weep and mourn over her; for no man buyeth their merchandise any more." Babylon will be the center of world trade. The ten-membered alliance of nations which forms a common market will be almost totally dependent upon political and economic Babylon. And suddenly she is gone.

WORLD COMMERCIAL CENTER

Listen to the goods symbolic Babylon deals in. Verses 12-13 indicate she trades in "The merchandise of gold, and silver, and precious stones, and pearls, and fine linen, and purple, and silk, and scarlet, and all thyine wood, and all kinds of vessels of ivory, and all kinds of vessels of most precious wood, and of bronze, and iron, and marble, And cinnamon, and incense, and ointments, and frankincense, and wine, and oil, and fine flour, and wheat, and cattle, and sheep, and horses, and chariots, and slaves, and souls of men." Beloved, everything from gold to the very bodies and souls of men and women are bought, sold and traded by the commercial activities of this great world center of the Antichrist.

For many months the world's merchants will have depended on economic Babylon and now what is left for them? Verses 15-16 give the answer. "The merchants of these things, who were made rich by her, shall stand afar off for the fear of her torment, weeping and wailing, And saying, Alas, alas (or Woe, woe) that great city, that was clothed in fine linen, and purple, and scarlet, and bedecked with gold, and precious stones, and pearls!" Commerce comes to an abrupt halt because the world center of trade is destroyed by God Himself.

Even "every shipmaster, and all the company in ships, and sailors, and as many as trade by sea, stood afar off, And cried when they saw the smoke of her burning, saying, What city is like unto this great city? And they cast dust on their heads, and cried, weeping and wailing, saying, Alas, alas, that great city, in which were made rich all that had ships in the sea by reason of her costliness! For in one hour is she made desolate." Verses 17-19.

The picture is clear. Antichrist will bring to an end the false system of religion centered in Rome (ecclesiastical Babylon) and then God will bring to an end the world commercial system centered in Rome (political Babylon). Both church and state will collapse. No more will man be able to appease himself with an easy, do-nothing religion. No more will he put his trust in world commerce and finance. The end of the Tribulation is near and man has only the lies of the Antichrist to cling to.

A CHANGE IN TONE

Suddenly and dramatically the whole tone of Revelation changes. Instead of weeping and wailing, instead of the fierceness of God's judgment on this wicked earth, there is the vibrant tone of rejoicing. Revelation 18:20-24 depicts the inhabitants of heaven rejoicing over the total destruction of Babylon in both her ecclesiastical and political forms. A mighty angel casts a great millstone into the sea, representing the final fall of Babylon. Verse 21. A dead silence arises from the now destroyed city. No more merriment, verse 22, no more wedding celebrations, verse 23, for the great harlot Babylon is destroyed forever.

The first ten verses of chapter 19 are closely linked to these events. Note that Revelation 19:1 begins with the words, "And after these things . . ." After the destruction of Babylon the whole tenor of Revelation becomes that of rejoicing for the King is coming. John hears "a great voice of many people in heaven, saying Hallelujah! Salvation, and glory, and honor, and power, unto the Lord, our God; For true and righteous are his judgments; for he hath judged the great harlot, who did corrupt the earth with her fornication, and hath avenged the blood of his servants at her hand." The song of praise by the angels, the twenty-four elders, the four living creatures and the multitudes of heaven includes praise for God's righteousness in judging Antichrist's evil system of worship as well as praise for avenging the blood of so many Tribulation believers martyred by Babylon.

THE HEAVENLY HALLELUJAH CHORUS

The end is near. Excitement and expectancy are in the air. John records, "And I heard, as it were, the voice of a great multitude, and like the voice of many waters, and like the voice of mighty peals of thunder, saying, Hallelujah! For the Lord God omnipotent reigneth." Verse 6. The great heavenly hallelujah chorus has begun.

In conjunction with this great sound of praise is the marriage supper of the Lamb. Gathered around the Lamb, the Lord Jesus Christ, are those who are His bride. Since the true Church of today is the Bride of Christ, this scene must take place in heaven. At the rapture of the Church, prior to the Tribulation period, we are joined in marriage to the Bridegroom — Jesus Christ. Now the wedding supper or feast (which always followed the wedding ceremony by a space of time) takes place.

In a joyous celebration, we who are the saints of God, raptured up to heaven before the Tribulation, stand before the Lord as bride before bridegroom arrayed "in fine linen, clean and white; for the fine linen is the righteousness of saints." Verse 8. Those of our labors for the Lord found worthy at the Judgment Seat of Christ now clothe us. And, from our vantage point in heaven, we join in praising the Lord of Glory, for the great harlot has been overthrown.

With this the stage is set for the most dramatic entrance in history. With the tone of Revelation changed from somber to jubilant, the way is prepared for the second coming of Christ. He is about to come as the KING OF KINGS AND LORD OF LORDS. What a joyous day that will be when the seven years of Tribulation are ended, judgment upon the earth is over, and Jesus Christ comes as the Prince of Peace to reign in peace.

THE SECOND COMING OF CHRIST

Chapter 19

Beloved, take a deep breath and sit back. We are about to consider the most mind-boggling event of history past, present or future. The great harlot Babylon is overthrown. There is fantastic rejoicing and praise in heaven for the blood of the saints is avenged. Yet this rejoicing only foreshadows the event which immediately follows — the second coming of Christ to this earth. No imagination can quite visualize this scene which the saints of all the ages have longingly anticipated. It is marvelous.

Christ first came to earth in the form of a babe in Bethlehem. There was no room for Him in the inn and thus He was born in a stable. His coming was on a quiet, silent night. He came to die for your sins and for mine. One day soon He will come again to lead all who know Him as Saviour to heaven. This event we refer to as the rapture or the "snatching away" of His true Church. He does not come to the earth at this time but only in the clouds where we are caught up to meet Him. His coming is accompanied with the sounding of trumpets, but all of this is heard only by those who are born-again believers.

But beloved, the event portrayed in Revelation 19 is neither the coming of the Lord as a babe or in the clouds to rapture His Church. This time He comes to earth again. It is His second coming to earth and He will do so as KING OF KINGS AND LORD OF LORDS. He will come to victoriously wage war against the beast and False Prophet. He will come to end the years of awful Tribulation. He will come as the Prince of Peace to reign in peace.

CHRIST RIDES FROM HEAVEN

In Revelation 19:11 John receives the vision of the second coming of Christ. He says, "And I saw heaven opened and, behold, a white horse; and he that sat upon him was called Faithful and True, and in righteousness he doth judge and make war." You can imagine that dramatic moment. Suddenly the heavens part, not to permit someone entrance, but to permit the Lord Jesus and His armies to ride out of heaven and do battle with the forces of Antichrist. As if the opening of heaven is not dramatic enough, Christ will ride a white horse through the opening in the skies but there will be no mistaking Him for the Antichrist who rode a white horse in Revelation 6:2. This is the real Conqueror. This is Christ, the Son of the living God.

Notice the graphic description of Jesus Christ in the next verses. "His eyes were like a flame of fire, and on his head were many crowns; and he had a name written, that no man knew, but he himself. And he was clothed with a vesture dipped in blood; and his name is called The Word of God . . . And out of his mouth goeth a sharp sword, that with it he should smite the nations, and he shall rule them with a rod of iron; and he treadeth the winepress of the fierceness and wrath of Almighty God. And he hath on his vesture and on his thigh a name written, KING OF KINGS, AND LORD OF LORDS." Verses 12-16. I don't know about you, but I get excited just reading about that.

PHYSICAL CHANGES IN THE EARTH

There are many other Scriptures in both the Old and New Testaments which anticipate this glorious coming of Christ. Zechariah 14:3-4 reveals, "Then shall the LORD go forth, and fight against those nations, as when he fought in the day of battle. And his feet shall stand in that day upon the Mount of Olives, which is before Jerusalem on the east, and the Mount of Olives shall cleave in its midst toward the east and toward the west, and there shall be a very great valley; and half of the mountain shall remove toward the north, and half of it toward the south."

Our Lord Himself tells of other startling phenomena which will accompany His return to this earth. He says, "Immediately after the tribulation of those days shall the sun be darkened, and the moon shall not give its light, and the stars shall fall from heaven, and the powers of the heavens shall be shaken. And then shall appear the sign of the Son of man in heaven; and then shall all the tribes of the earth mourn, and they shall see the Son of man coming in the clouds of heaven with power and great glory." Matt. 24:29-30.

With the heavens opening as a scroll, the plea of Isaiah is fulfilled. The ancient prophet pleaded, "Oh, that thou wouldest rend the heavens, that thou wouldest come down, that the mountains might flow down at thy presence, As when the melting fire burneth, and the fire causeth the waters to boil, to make thy name known to thine adversaries, that the nations may tremble at thy presence." Isa. 64:1-2.

THE FOWL'S FEAST OF FLESH

Christ Jesus comes to earth this second time to establish a thousand year reign of righteousness. But before He can do this, the forces of evil, led by the Antichrist, must be defeated on the battlefield. Beginning with Revelation 19:17 John previews this great battle. An angel standing in the light of the sun with a loud voice invites the fowls that fly in the midst of the heavens to "Come and gather yourselves together unto the supper of the great God, That ye may eat the flesh of kings, and the flesh of captains, and the flesh of mighty men, and the flesh of horses and of them that sit on them, and the flesh of all men, both free and enslaved, both small and great."

The angel, of course, has reference to the carrion and carnage of the great battle about to take place. So mighty is the Lord in battle that it will take a multitude of fowl to clean up the battlefield upon which His enemies die.

The reason for this battle is simple. Antichrist blasphemes the name of God, lies, cheats, and deceives his way into world leadership. He institutes a false system of religion in which he is the center of worship. When in the middle of the Tribulation the Jews no longer can freely worship God, they flee to the safety of the wilderness. Antichrist is unsuccessful in destroying them. Rev. 12:15-16. His own capital city of Babylon falls as a result of the direct judgment from God. Rev. 18. Only one group of people remains against whom Antichrist can vent his wrath, and that is a small band of Jews bottled up in the city of Jerusalem. These "Keep the commandments of God, and have the testimony of Jesus Christ" (12:17) and become the object of Antichrist's hatred. Zechariah 14:1-2 indicates that all the nations of the earth, who comprise the armies of the world ruler, will be gathered against Jerusalem to battle. It is then the clouds part and King Jesus Christ rides forth with His armies.

ARMAGEDDON

This will be the most spectacular battle in history. In his vision of the coming battle, Revelation 16:13-16, John tells us that Antichrist's troops are mustered by three demons who, like frogs, come out of the mouth of Satan, Antichrist and the False Prophet. The troops are gathered together in a place called in the Hebrew tongue Armageddon. This site, which means "the mountain of Megiddo," is adjacent to the plain of Megiddo on the west and the large plain of Esdraelon on the northeast. Here was the scene of many great battles in the Old Testament. Judges 4 and 7.

Although the armies of the nations will be deployed over an area of nearly 200 miles (Rev. 14:20) and some troops will be fighting directly against Jerusalem (Zech. 14:2), the focal point of the battle will be Armageddon. The valley of Esdraelon (Jezreel) is itself fourteen miles wide and twenty miles long and the blood from the killed and wounded will run to the bridles of the horses. Rev. 14:20.

When the forces of Antichrist ride against the KING OF KINGS and His armies, there will be no contest. The King is armed only with the sharp sword that goes out of His mouth, and by the power of the Word of God the evil armies are slain. The battle of Armageddon is swift and deadly. The remnant of Antichrist's army is slain by Him that "sat upon the horse, which sword proceeded out of his mouth; and all fowls were filled with their flesh." Rev. 19:21.

Friends, when the KING OF KINGS AND LORD OF LORDS rides forth out of heaven, followers of Antichrist become a meal for the fowls of the air. The flesh of kings, captains, military men, and horses, the flesh of free men, enslaved men, small and great men will be served up for these fowls. This repulsive gory sight will result from judgment, the proportions of which the world has never seen before. The victory of Christ Jesus will be total over the world who despised Him.

ENEMIES VANQUISHED

At the consummation of this great battle the enemies of Christ are vanquished. Their leaders, the Antichrist and False Prophet are "cast alive into a lake of fire burning with brimstone." Verse 20. Note that only these two are cast into the lake of fire and precede Satan himself into this place of everlasting punishment by a thousand years. Rev. 20:10. These two men, the civil and religious leaders of the league of nations against God, are cast alive into this horrible torment where a thousand years later they are still said to be suffering the vengeance of eternal fire. This should indicate beyond a doubt that the lake of fire is not annihilation and is not purgatory. It neither annihilates nor purifies these two but torments them eternally.

The Bible is plain. "For God so loved the world, that he gave his only begotten Son, that whosoever believeth in him should not perish, but have everlasting life. For God sent not his Son into the world to condemn the world, but that the world through him might be saved." John 3:16-17. All who avail themselves of this grace of God and receive the atonement of His Son on the cross of Calvary will be given a blessed eternity in heaven with God. On the other hand, those who spurn God's grace must be aware they will face Christ in judgment. They will be His conquered enemy without hope of eternal life in heaven. Friends, it is very foolish to read only those portions of God's Word which speak of His love and grace and not consider those which speak of the sure judgment to come on those who reject Jesus as Saviour. Ride with Him out of the heavens in victory or face Him in battle as enemy. The choice is yours. **"Believe on the Lord Jesus Christ, and thou shalt be saved, and thy house."** Acts 16:31.

Friday 8-18-06

NEXT

THE MILLENNIUM AND GREAT WHITE THRONE JUDGMENT

Chapter 20

After seven long and increasingly severe years, the Tribulation is over. Christ Jesus comes to earth again and the forces of Antichrist are defeated in the awesome battle of Armageddon. Now comes the calm after the storm. Chapter 20 of Revelation informs us of the one thousand year reign of Christ on this earth, known as the Millennium. Once again this planet will return to an atmosphere similar to the Garden of Eden and the reason is simple. In the first three verses, John sees an angel coming down from heaven with the key to the bottomless pit and a chain in his hand. The angel seizes the dragon, that old serpent the devil, and binds him for a thousand years, casting him into the bottomless pit, shutting him up and sealing him there. All of this is done to prevent Satan from deceiving the nations till the thousand years is fulfilled. After that, the devil is again loosed for **"a little season."**

ONE THOUSAND YEAR REIGN

Now you may say, "Brother Kroll, how do you know that it will actually be one thousand years Christ Jesus reigns in peace and righteousness? This is the only chapter in the Bible that mentions a millennium or thousand-year reign." Yes, that's correct. But how many times does God have to say it to make it so? Once should be enough. But note here, He repeats it six times. Verses 2,3,4,5,6 and 7 all refer to the period of a thousand years. Friends, this is a literal, thousand-year era when the Lord of Glory will be the King of the earth.

Multitudes of people shall enter the Millennium. New Testament saints, you and I — the Church, will rule and reign along with Christ. Rev. 3:21. Old Testament saints shall rule in some sense as well. Other saints will now be resurrected to reign with Christ. Rev. 20:4,6. Great numbers of the nation of Israel shall enter the millennial kingdom: the 144,000 (Rev. 14:3-4), those who flee into the wilderness hideaway (Rev. 12:6) and those who remain in Jerusalem. Rev. 12:17. Millions of Gentiles who are saved during the Tribulation shall enter the kingdom. Matt. 24:31-34. But no unsaved person shall enter the millennial kingdom of Christ. Matt. 13:41-43; 49-50; 25:41,46.

YEARS OF PEACE

With the Antichrist and False Prophet in the lake of fire and Satan bound in the bottomless pit, this will be an idyllic place to live. In his vision, John does not occupy himself with the details of the millennial kingdom — only that it is one thousand years in length. However, many Old Testament passages describe this blessed reign of Christ. Isaiah 2:2-4 indicates that Jerusalem will be the Lord's capital city and the center of the world. Also, now the world will see for the first time what the United Nations spends millions of dollars each year searching for, but never finding. I speak of worldwide peace, under the administration of the Prince of Peace. Isaiah 2:4 says, "And he shall judge among the nations, and shall rebuke many peoples; and they shall beat their swords into plowshares, and their spears into pruning hooks; nation shall not lift up sword against nation, neither shall they learn war any more." Mark it down, friends. There will be no world peace until the millennial kingdom of Christ, for there can be no peace apart from Him. Isaiah 11 describes the peace and tranquility of Christ's kingdom. "The wolf also shall dwell with the lamb, and the leopard shall lie down with the kid; and the calf and the young lion and the fatling together, and a little child shall lead them. And the nursing child shall play on the hole of the asp, and the weaned child shall put his hand on the adder's den." Verses 6 and 8.

During the blissful one thousand year reign of Christ, this earth will have a perfect physical environment. It will also have a perfect spiritual environment because Satan is no longer free to deceive the inhabitants of this planet. It will have a perfect moral environment because the sovereign of this kingdom is Christ Himself. Psalm 2:6-9.

SATAN LOOSED

However, at the end of the thousand years, Satan will be loosed from the bottomless pit and again deceive the nations, gathering them together for battle. Rev. 20:7-8. Now you ask, "How can there be any who follow Satan if all who enter the Millennium are washed clean in the blood of the Lamb?" Well, though all who enter Christ's kingdom know and love the Lord, soon children will be born to these believing parents. Over the course of a thousand years you can see that hundreds of thousands of children will be born. Because Christ rules in righteousness with a rod of iron, they will worship Him on the outside but not all will worship Him in their hearts. Those who do not come to truly love the Lord during the Millennium will be gathered by Satan at the end of the thousand years in one final, desperate attempt to usurp the throne of God. As in all other attempts, they will be unsuccessful, for God will send fire from heaven and devour them. Verse 9.

Thus, the millennial reign of Christ illustrates two things. First, having a perfect environment doesn't make a sinner into a saint. Those born in the Millennium have the most ideal environment imaginable. There is no war, no famine, no moral corruption. Still, they rally around the devil when he is finally loosed. Second, having a perfect heredity doesn't make a sinner into a saint. Each of these born during the reign of Christ are born to Christian parents. But believing parents do not make a believing child. Children of these millennial saints, numbering as the sands of the sea, turn against God the first chance they get. Why is this? It is because of the sinful nature which is part of every human being. Everyone, even those born to believers in the Millennium, must recognize his individual responsibility to receive Jesus Christ as his Saviour from sin.

With Satan's final armies purged from the earth by fire, Satan is himself now cast into the lake of fire and brimstone where the beast and False Prophet are. Verse 10. Now, please note something. Satan, the Antichrist and the False Prophet "shall be tormented day and night forever and ever." Beloved, there is no more graphic way of saying that hell or the lake of fire is a place of torment which lasts forever. The cults are wrong when they say death is annihilation. The scoffers are wrong when they say they will enjoy hell with their friends. Hell is sheer torment forever and ever.

GREAT WHITE THRONE JUDGMENT

Immediately after John views Satan being cast into the lake of fire, he receives another vision. This time it is of a Great White Throne. There have been other thrones mentioned in this book but none are like this one. It is pure white, the type of white that makes everything else look dirty. Only the wicked — the unsaved — will appear before this throne of judgment. Unbelievers will have no difficulty in seeing their sin when they stand before the Great White Throne. The one who sits upon this throne is undoubtedly the Lord Jesus Christ for "the Father judgeth no man, but hath committed all judgment unto the Son." John 5:22.

Verse 11 contains a curious reference to the fact that from the face of Christ "the earth and the heaven fled away, and there was found no place for them." The most natural interpretation of this is that now the present heaven and earth are destroyed and replaced by the new heaven and new earth. The Bible frequently anticipates the time when this present world will be destroyed. Matt. 24:35; II Pet. 3:10.

Those who stand before the Great White Throne are the "dead, small and great." Verse 12. As they appear before God, a single book and many books are opened and they are judged according to their works. Now, what can these books be? Well, the single book is identified by the verse. It is the Lamb's book of life. Here are recorded the names of the elect from before the foundation of the world. A careful search is now made to be absolutely certain that the names of none of these unsaved people standing before the Great White Throne are in the book of life. None are, for God keeps careful records and knows who are His own. Not one person judged here has received Christ as Saviour. These are the wicked who have died in ages past, now resurrected to be judged.

Next, the many books are checked to see the works of these who are to be judged. This is not the book of life, but books recording the deeds of the wicked. They are condemned by the fact that their name is not in the book of life. But the degree of punishment they receive for eternity is decided by the amount and atrocity of their deeds here on earth. *Sunday August 20-06*

Next — THE LAKE OF FIRE

As a result of this Great White Throne Judgment "death and hades were cast into the lake of fire. This is the second death. And whosoever was not found written in the book of life was cast into the lake of fire." Rev. 20:14-15.

Some of your Bibles may say "death and hell." This should not be translated in this manner. No one ever returns from hell. Death claims the body and may be referred to as the ground. Hades claims the soul and is an intermediate state for the wicked until they are raised at the Great White Throne. Hell is the lake of fire and in these verses John indicates that death gives up the wickeds' bodies and hades gives up the wickeds' souls so that they may be properly judged and together cast into hell, the lake of fire. This means that the death that unsaved men die on earth is only temporary. All will one day be raised and judged. Since their names are not in the book of life, they cannot inherit eternal life. What they do inherit is the second death. From this final death there is no resurrection. It is eternal separation from God in the darkness and punishment of hell. When the wicked die the first time, their fate is sealed. There is no second chance. When the dead are raised at the end of the Millennium and stand before the Great White Throne

Judgment, they receive the fruit of their wicked deeds and rejection of Christ. The wages of sin is death — eternal death, separation from God and everything desirable, forever.

Friend, the only way to escape this eternal punishment is by receiving Jesus Christ as Saviour. He died so that you may live. It is true that "the wages of sin is death" but the verse continues, "the gift of God is eternal life through Jesus Christ, our Lord." Rom. 6:23. You may enjoy life eternal by faith in Jesus Christ. With Him you inherit eternal life and heaven. Without Him you inherit eternal death and hell. I beg you to receive His shed blood on the cross as payment for the wages of your sin. "That if thou shalt confess with thy mouth the Lord Jesus, and shalt believe in thine heart that God hath raised him from the dead, thou shalt be saved . . . For whosoever shall call upon the name of the Lord shall be saved." Rom. 10:9 and 13.

THE NEW HEAVEN AND NEW EARTH
Chapter 21

With the Great White Throne Judgment, the thousand-year reign of Christ on this earth comes to an end. The Millennium, with its peace and tranquility, is certainly an improvement over our world today. It's hard to believe that anything can be better than this reign of peace. However, when Christ's thousand-year reign comes to a close, the Millennium merges with eternity and no matter how you look at it there is nothing better than heaven.

In chapter 21 John sees "a new heaven and a new earth; for the first heaven and the first earth were passed away, and there was no more sea."

A NEW WORLD ORDER

Friends, when God sends a new heaven and a new earth, He doesn't just clean up our polluted streams and rivers. He doesn't simply remake this old planet by knocking off some rough edges. He doesn't renovate the earth. God makes a new earth as He does a new heaven. In verse 5 He says, "Behold, I make all things new."

When God saved me He didn't just patch me up, wash me off, make me over and reform me. Not at all. He made me a new creature, a new created being. Old things passed completely away and all things became new. II Cor. 5:17. This is what He will one day do to heaven and earth. **"Heaven and earth shall pass away"** our Lord tells us. Matt. 24:35. The Apostle Peter writes, "But the day of the Lord will come as a thief in the night, in which the heavens shall pass away with a great noise, and the elements shall melt with fervent heat; the earth also, and the works that are in it, shall be burned up.

Seeing, then, that all these things shall be dissolved, what manner of persons ought ye to be in all holy living and godliness, Looking for and hasting unto the coming of the day of God, in which the heavens, being on fire, shall be dissolved, and the elements shall melt with fervent heat? Nevertheless we, according to his promise, look for new heavens and a new earth, in which dwelleth righteousness." II Pet. 3:10-13.

The Bible doesn't say much about how this new earth will look, but we know there will be no more seas to separate people. Men and women will be able to roam this new earthly paradise uninhibitedly. It will be far more beautiful than we can conceive.

THE NEW JERUSALEM

Likewise, the new Jerusalem, the holy city, is seen by John "coming down from God out of heaven, prepared as a bride adorned for her husband." Rev. 20:2. With the descent of the new Jerusalem, we are placed in an even more desirable relationship with God than we have ever had. Verse 3 tells us, "God is with men, and he will dwell with them, and they shall be his people, and God himself shall be with them, and be their God." Just think! God the Son came to dwell among men in order to save them. John 1:14. God the Spirit came to dwell among men in order to comfort them. John 14:16-18. Now God the Father comes to dwell among men in order to fellowship with them.

The environment of the new Jerusalem will even be better than that of the Millennium, for God will exclude from entrance "the fearful, and unbelieving, and the abominable, and murderers, and fornicators, and sorcerers, and idolaters, and all liars." Verse 8. It is important to note that those people who are excluded are people whose lives are characterized by these sinful traits. They will be cast into the lake of fire, indicating they are wicked unbelievers. It does not say that anyone who has ever committed any of these sins will be excluded. There is a great difference between telling a lie and being a habitual liar. Neither are commendable but the believer can confess his sin and have it forgiven. The unbeliever is hardened into a life style which is characteristic of his unbelief. Only the unbeliever is excluded from the new Jerusalem.

The new heaven, the holy city, is so fantastically beautiful it almost defies words. However, under the guidance of the Holy Spirit, John attempts a description in Revelation 21. Let's note how he describes it.

WORLD'S LARGEST METROPOLIS

First, it is a literal city "coming down from God out of heaven." Verse 2. Verse 10 repeats saying it is a "great city, the holy Jerusalem, descending out of heaven from God." It is important to note that nowhere is the city said to rest upon the new earth. It comes down or descends from God out of heaven and apparently hovers over the new earth. The city itself is immense. **"And the city lieth foursquare, and the length is as large as the breadth; and he (John) measured the city with the reed, twelve thousand furlongs. The length and the breadth and the height of it are equal."** Verse 16. A furlong is about 600 feet which means that the new Jerusalem is roughly 1,500 miles long, 1,500 miles wide and 1,500 miles high.

Now, beloved, think a minute. Here is a city which covers an area of 1,500 miles by 1,500 miles or 2,250,000 square miles. This means that the base of the new Jerusalem is more than eight times the size of the entire state of Texas or two-thirds the size of the United States. And in addition to that, it towers 1,500 miles straight up as a gigantic skyscraper. It is of fantastic proportions and certainly capable of housing the Bride of Christ.

Although not greatly important, the shape of this city must either be a pyramid or a cube. Perhaps it is best to think of it as a cube for this shape is frequently seen in the Scriptures. Both the altar of burnt offering and the altar of incense were of this form. Ex. 27:1; 30:2. The Holy of Holies in Solomon's Temple was a perfect cube, 20 cubits each way. I Kings 6:20. Even the Greeks thought this shape to be a symbol of perfection.

TWELVE GATES

The glory of God permeates the city. Around it is a wall great and high having twelve gates with an angel posted at each gate. Verse 12. The names written on the gates are of the twelve tribes of Israel, perhaps to remind each of us who dwell therein that we owe our Bible, our Saviour and much more to Israel. "Salvation is of the Jews." John 4:22. Each of the gates is made of one giant pearl. Verse 21. This should remind us, by the very process needed to make a pearl, that much suffering was undergone in order to provide an entrance into the holy city. Jesus Christ said, "I am the door; by me if any man enter in, he shall be saved, and shall go in and out, and find pasture." John 10:9. In order to become the door the Lord had to suffer the anguish of dying on the cross. "But he was wounded for our transgressions, he was bruised for our iniquities; the chastisement for our peace was upon him, and with his stripes we are healed." Isa. 53:5. Yes, friend, Jesus paid a great price to be the door of our salvation. He suffered immensely and it is altogether fitting that the gates into the new Jerusalem be of pearl.

TWELVE FOUNDATIONS

The foundations of the city number twelve as well and each one bears the name of one of the twelve apostles of the Lamb. Perhaps this is to remind us that the Church began with these men. Eph. 2:20. Each of the foundations is garnished with all manner of precious stones. The first is clear jasper. The second a brilliant blue sapphire. The third a sky-blue chalcedony. The fourth a bright green emerald. The fifth a red and white sardonyx. The sixth a reddish sardius stone. The seventh a transparent golden chrysolyte. The eighth a sea-green beryl. The ninth a transparent yellow-green topaz. The tenth a green chrysoprasus. The eleventh a violet jacinth. And the twelfth a purple amethyst. Each one contributing to the unimaginable beauty of this holy city.

The whole city is described as being of "pure gold, like clear glass." Verse 18. Even the street of the city is pure gold, as transparent glass. Now you know that gold is a most precious and most expensive commodity. Yet the city foursquare is lavishly made from pure gold, indicating an abode fit to be the dwelling place of God.

THINGS ABSENT FROM THE NEW CITY

With the description of the magnificence displayed by this city, you may wonder if there is anything not included in the new Jerusalem. Yes, there is. You'll recall that verse 4 indicates that "God shall wipe away all tears from their eyes; and there shall be no more death, neither sorrow, nor crying, neither shall there be any more pain; for the former things are passed away." Do you think you'll be able to get along without these things in heaven? You won't miss them for a minute.

But note, verses 22 and following indicate additional things that won't be in the new city of God. John saw no temple there **"for the Lord God Almighty and the Lamb are the temple of it. And the city had no need of the sun, neither of the moon, to shine in it; for the glory of God did light it, and the Lamb is the lamp of it."**

This thought is repeated in chapter 22, verse 5. Also chapter 22, verse 3, indicates that "there shall be no more curse, but the throne of God and of the Lamb shall be in it, and his servants shall serve him."

Have you ever wondered what we will do in heaven? Listen, friends, heaven is not a place to sit around under a shade tree, play a harp and be bored all day long. With God in our midst we will have the capacity to know Him more, love Him more and serve Him more. There will be plenty to do in heaven and it will cause unimaginable joy. Even those living on the new earth, who seem to be redeemed Israel (Rom. 4:13) and the saved multitudes who come out of the Millennium, will have access to the holy city and "the nations of them who are saved shall walk in the light of it, and the kings of the earth do bring their glory and honor into it. And the gates of it shall not be shut at all by day; for there shall be no night there. And they shall bring the glory and honor of the nations into it." Rev. 21:24-26. A river of life, clear as crystal, will proceed out of the throne of God and the Lamb— and spanning the river the tree of life which bears twelve kinds of fruits year round will maintain the health of the nations on the new earth. Rev. 22:1-2.

Beloved, briefly this is a description of what awaits us in the new Jerusalem. Perhaps I can best describe our future eternal home with the sentiments of Isaiah and the Apostle Paul. "Eye hath not seen, nor ear heard, neither have entered into the heart of man, the things which God hath prepared for them that love him." Isa. 64:4; I Cor. 2:9. Praise God, Hallelujah. I'm a child of the King.

THE FINAL MESSAGE OF THE BIBLE
Chapter 22

With Chapter 22 the Apostle John completes his commissioned task to "write the things which thou hast seen, and the things which are, and the things which shall be hereafter." Rev. 1:19. His visions come to a glorious end. The last few verses of Revelation seem to be given as reinforcement that what John has seen will certainly come to pass. Revelation 22:6 indicates, "These words are faithful and true; and the Lord God of the holy prophets sent his angel to show unto his servants the things which must shortly be done."

That the words recorded in Revelation are true is seen in that they are statements of fact given from the lips of God Himself. That they are faithful is evident in that they will surely come to pass. There is no question in John's mind about this and there should be none in ours as well.

VISION REVIEW

John has envisioned being caught up into heaven to view the opening of the seven-sealed scroll, the sounding of the seven trumpets and the pouring out of the seven bowls of God's wrath. He has seen the awful Tribulation period to come and in the middle of that period the rise of the Antichrist and the False Prophet. He has seen multitudes slain for the testimony of the Gospel and other multitudes receive the mark of the beast. He has viewed the rise and destruction of the Antichrist's capital city, symbolically known as Babylon the harlot. He has seen the ecumenical movement at its height and the collapse of the one-world church. He has seen the common market nations economically fall apart at the hand of God. And at the end of the Tribulation John has viewed the second coming of Christ to the earth. The KING

OF KINGS AND LORD OF LORDS has ridden forth as the heavens opened and has conquered the forces of Antichrist at the fierce battle of Armageddon. John watched as Antichrist and the False Prophet were cast into the lake of fire.

Then John saw something truly amazing. He viewed Christ as the King of the earth, ruling in righteousness and peace for one thousand years. He saw a society more blissful than any of history. But at the end of this thousand-year reign he saw Satan, loosed from the bottomless pit, spearhead a thwarted coup of God's kingdom and then be cast into the lake of fire to be tormented day and night forever. Likewise those who have rejected Christ as Saviour were raised from the dead and judged at the Great White Throne Judgment. They, too, were cast into the lake of fire to be tormented forever and ever.

At this point John received his first glimpse of eternity. The heaven and earth were completely created new and a new city of Jerusalem descended from God out of heaven. It was more beautiful than John could adequately describe. Time was now swallowed up in eternity and John's vision was about to come to an end. Before it does he is assured that the vision is accurate and the Lord will quickly be returning to inaugurate these events. Rev. 22:7.

GOD ALONE WORTHY OF WORSHIP

John is overawed by what he has just witnessed and heard and falls down to worship before the feet of the angel who has shown him these things. The angel rebukes him, however, saying that he is but John's fellow servant and that John should only worship God. Rev. 22:9. Beloved, this is good advice for all of us to heed. Frequently as believers we tend to praise the man who brings us the Gospel and neglect to praise the God who instituted the Gospel. We may appreciate pastors, radio preachers, Bible conference speakers, etc., but they must never become the object of our worship. God alone is worthy of our worship, and we must only give it to Him.

In verse 10, John is commanded not to seal the words of the prophecy of this book. The reason is clear. There is blessing for anyone who keeps the sayings of the prophecies given in Revelation. Rev. 22:7. Besides, the time is near when the Lord will come quickly, and people will need to understand what God is doing for them. (cf. Dan. 12:4). The time period which will usher in the eternal state is very near and in John's day as in ours the end is always impending because Christ may return at any moment, and the timepiece of Revelation will start ticking away. Therefore, this book is to be opened, read, heeded as a source of blessing.

Verses 11 through 15 seem to be a unit describing the sealing of one's destiny when the Lord comes. At that time all who are unjust will remain so, all filthy will continue to be filthy, all that are righteous will be righteous still and all who live holy lives will continue to do so. When the Lord Jesus comes to snatch His bride away, before the beginning of the Tribulation, He will then reward the saints according to their works. Salvation is a free gift that cannot be earned. But rewards are given in a response to faithful service. At the rapture not only will all opportunity for salvation be gone for unbelievers of this age, but also all opportunity for earthly service to the Lord will be gone for believers. Beloved, what you are going to do for the Lord must be done now. Your eternal reward depends on your service to Him presently, and He warns each of us that He is coming quickly.

ALPHA AND OMEGA

That this is true is confirmed by the one who makes the claim to be coming quickly. He is Jesus Christ the Lord and identifies Himself saying, "I am **Alpha and Omega, the beginning and the end, the first and the last.**" Verse 13. Alpha and Omega are the first and last letters of the Greek alphabet. In other words, Jesus is all and in all. He is the beginning of this revelation and the end of it. He is the complete One. What He says is to be believed.

Additional titles of the Alpha and Omega are given in verse 16. As if to personally assure us of the authenticity of

His revelation to John, He says, "I, Jesus, have sent mine angel to testify unto you these things in the churches. I am the root and the offspring of David, and the bright and morning star." I think it is significant that this is the first time the word "church" occurs in Revelation since the third chapter. All during the Tribulation chapters (4-19) there is no mention of the Church since as born-again believers we are caught up to be with the Lord before the awful period of judgment begins.

As the offspring of David the Lord Jesus shows His divine right to sit upon the throne as KING OF KINGS AND LORD OF LORDS for all eternity. As the bright and morning star He shall be our light in the new heaven and new earth for "there shall be no night there; and they need no lamp neither light of the sun; for the Lord God giveth them light, and they shall reign forever and ever." Rev. 22:5.

GOD'S FINAL CALL

At this point, realizing that although what John is recording is in the future it will be read in our present age, God issues a final call for the unsaved to receive Him. Isn't that just like our God? "And the Spirit and the bride say, Come. And let him that heareth say, Come. And let him that is athirst come. And whosoever will, let him take the water of life freely." Verse 17. A similar call is extended in Isaiah 55:1 but because the hour of judgment is impending, the call is now ever so much more serious.

Friend, someday you'll hear God's final call to you. If you receive Christ Jesus as Saviour and accept His sacrifice on the cross as payment for your sins, then you have a home in heaven with God throughout eternity. If you reject Him you may be assured of the eternal torment which is caused by the lake of fire. God calls, I relay His call, but only you can answer that call. One day I did and my life was completely changed. I was born again. That same experience can be yours today. Won't you heed His call? Won't you ask Christ Jesus to forgive you of your sin and come into your life and cleanse it? You will never regret seriously considering and answering God's call to eternal life.

GOD'S FINAL WARNING

Verses 18 and 19 of Revelation 22 contain a stern warning about adding to or taking away from the words of the prophecy of this book. Beloved, anyone who changes these words or their meanings, anyone who claims they are not the words of God or that they are just myth, anyone who attempts to add to them is promised the plagues written in this book will afflict them. God shall take away their part from the tree of life and the holy city. Now this doesn't mean they will lose their salvation, for anyone who would attempt such a crime is undoubtedly not a believer anyway. Only an unregenerated sinner would attempt to deny the Word or add to the Word of God. Friend, remember. Anyone who comes to your door and says you need their book or study guide in addition to the Bible is a person contemptible to God and condemned in these verses. The Bible alone is the Word of God. You need nothing in addition to it to be a guide for your life. No additions or deletions are desirable or acceptable.

EVEN SO, COME

Finally, John concludes the record of the Revelation by repeating the words of Jesus Christ — "Surely, I come quickly. Amen." Verse 20. This is similar to the expressions found in verses 7 and 12 but with the noticeable addition of the word "surely." This is the final testimony of Christ to us. His return for us is imminent. It could be today. John felt that way when he breathed the prayer, "Even so, come, Lord Jesus."

This is the Revelation of Jesus Christ telling us of events which must shortly come to pass. My prayer is that of John, "Even so, come, Lord Jesus" for the sooner He comes and takes me from this messed up old world the sooner the events of Revelation take place and I can begin enjoying eternity in the holy city, the new Jerusalem.

Friends, we have come to the close of the Book of Revelation but our study has brought us to the beginning of eternal life with God. We haven't ended, we've only just begun. History has ended. Life with Jesus Christ our Lord has not. We have nothing to look forward to but endless ages of joy in the presence of our Saviour. "Even so, come, Lord Jesus."

The Beginning

Finished reading on August 21-06

Bill 8-21-06

"Even so Come Lord Jesus"